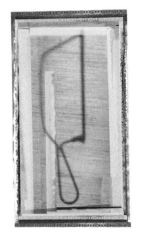

The Career Fix-It Book

How to Make Your Job Work Better For You

Diana Pace, PH.D.

Published by Sourcebooks, Inc.
P.O. Box 4410, Naperville, Illinois 60567-4410
(630) 961-3900
FAX: 630-961-2168

Library of Congress Cataloging-in-Publication Data
Pace, Diana.
    The career fix-it book: how to make your job work better for you / Diana Pace.
        p. cm.
    ISBN 1-57071-562-9 (alk. paper)
    1.Career changes. 2. Career development. I. Title.

    HF5384.P33 2000
        650.14—dc21

                                                                00-044038

Printed and bound in the United States of America

DR   10 9 8 7 6 5 4 3 2 1

Dedication

To my mother and father, Nell and Bus Graham, and my aunt, Elizabeth Gibson, who taught me the joy of living.

Acknowledgments

I would like to acknowledge first of all my partner and editor, Kathleen Blumreich, who was able to make sense out of what I was trying to say—no easy task. Her ability to turn complicated and confusing ideas into understandable, useful information is remarkable. Thank you, Kathleen.

I would also like to acknowledge my friend, Dotti Clune. She is coach and organizer par excellence. She kept me on task, helped me to figure out how to find a publisher, and always had a positive and encouraging word of support.

Thanks, too, to family members who took the time to provide encouragement and assistance: Matthew Guma, Cile Pace, Susan Guma, Jane Pace, Tom Pace, and Anne Pace.

Finally, I would like to acknowledge my colleagues at Grand Valley State University who read the manuscript and provided useful feedback: Cameron Dean, Sharon Helgert, Wayne Kinzie, Joan Lester, Patrick McGrath, Bart Merkle, Sharon Mills, Barbara Palombi, Janet Potgeter, Harriet Singleton, and John Zaugra.

And to my lifelong friends, Dorothy Berg and Phyllis Lane, who believe in me *and* make me laugh—the best qualities possible in friends—thank you for your confidence.

Contents

A Buddhist priest named Thin Nat Han, wrote a book called *Zen Mind, Beginners Mind*. In it, he encouraged the reader to approach tasks as a beginner. Beginners, he explained, come to a task without habits, strong opinions from previous experiences, or a kind of "know it all" attitude. Their approach is fresh and unencumbered. This is the approach that I want you to consider in examining your career plans.

Chapter One

Clear Out the Cobwebs

"You can't steal second if you never take off from first."
–Chris Rocca

In order to take a fresh look at what is wrong (or right) in your work life, it is important to clear out old misconceptions. The problem with misconceptions is that they tend to be automatic; that is, we include them in our thinking without realizing it. Consider, for example, driving in England. In order to shift to driving on the left side of the road, it is necessary to think about driving on it. Otherwise, we will automatically drive on the right side. As with driving, we have developed particular habits or notions about ourselves and our careers. Our thinking may be accurate (driving on the right side) or it may be inaccurate (driving on the right side in England). But without examining our assumptions in a very conscious way, we cannot expect to proceed with making good career decisions for the future. Our pasts exert a strong influence on us, and although I'm not Freud, I do agree with him that the unconscious or subconscious (what we assume but are not consciously aware of) often guides our choices.

You are going to review all of your notions about career and bring them out for "airing" to determine if they still are true for you. The best place to start is at the beginning. I'm going to ask you to go way back to when you first started thinking about work. You may have only been five years old and that's OK. Try to recall what you wanted to be when you "grew up." Clues can be found in the kinds of things you did when you were young—your favorite activities, games, etc. A good friend of mine who is an excellent writer today loved to write stories when she was little. My brother, who used to follow my father around begging to go to work with him, eventually worked for the very same paving and construction company. My daughter easily put together crossword puzzles. She now works in a DNA lab.

Some activities were not perhaps your most favorite. I took piano lessons for twelve years, disliked every minute of it, and can't play a single piece today. My mother had every hope that I would become a famous musician. Both my feelings about music and her efforts to "push" me are important for me to be aware of because both have influenced me. Going to the symphony is a love of mine that grew out of my piano lessons. I just don't have any talent for or interest in creating the music myself.

Have a serious look at what you loved—and didn't love—when you were young. I think you will be surprised to find many nuggets of information that can explain who you are today. You will then have the advantage of your life history before you, and you can pull information from that as you begin to examine your current career plans.

Take a few moments to do the following exercise.

Exercise

What Did I Want to Be When I Grew Up?

1) Think of your earliest idea of what you wanted to be. What age were you approximately? Continue with the rest of the exercise, then, in the lines provided under each item, add why each of these choices held some appeal for you. What were the reasons for being attracted to these particular choices? Excitement? A parent's career? Status?

Career_____ Age_____

_____

_____

_____

_____

2) Continue with your other career ideas and provide a list of these with approximate ages.

Career_____ Age_____

_____

_____

_____

_____

Career_____ Age_____

_____

_____

_____

Career_____ Age_____

_____

_____

_____

Career_____ Age_____

_____

_____

_____

Career_____ Age_____

_____

_____

_____

Career_____ Age_____

_____

_____

_____

Now, go back and circle those careers and reasons that still ring true for you or have some kind of appeal. It may be all, some, or none of them.

Exercise

Who Influenced Me in My Past?

All of us receive pressure from others and our environment as we grow up regarding what we should do with our lives. Typically, this pressure comes from parents, but well-meaning relatives, teachers, and friends also can be sources of this kind of advice. Even absence of advice can have meaning. Young people who are not encouraged to think about college get a clear message that a degree is worthless, and thus may not be likely to pursue higher education.

Write down those life career choices (including homemaking and parenting) that you were supposed to go into, for what reasons, and who gave you this advice.

Career or Life Activity	Reasons	Person Who Encouraged This

Exercise

Present Influences

Now, put yourself back in the present. Although you have matured and developed your own ideas and preferences as you have grown up, still there can be people and experiences in your adult life that exert influence on you. You may not even be aware of what these influences are without giving them some conscious thought. But unless we bring these influences out in the open, we cannot measure their effect. Nor can we determine to what degree they fit who we are. We don't live in a vacuum, and our daily decisions are not just the result of our own wants and needs, but are influenced by our environment.

Our decisions are based largely on our priorities and not necessarily what we want at all. My favorite activity was water skiing when I was younger. I still love it. But I find that I am considering buying an electric motor boat—which probably wouldn't even pull a small child on an innertube, much less me on skis. Why would I override my own love of an activity? Because the electric motor doesn't produce smoke and noise. All of the "save the environment" information has influenced me. Even more related to career choices is the example of a colleague of mine who loves to watch sports on TV. She has chosen to work only half-time in her job because she wants to watch as many professional sports games as possible. She knows that by doing so, her "career ladder" is limited, but she is willing to make that sacrifice. Fortunately, she has a husband who can fill in the income necessary for them to have an adequate living.

What forces, both internal and external, currently influence your career choices? Think about what factors most greatly weigh on you when it comes to career choice. It may be your own desires or doubts, pressure from family, or a current work situation. Write down each of these factors, what the message is, and who is saying it.

Current factors or people influencing career choice	Reasons	Factors/persons, including yourself, who are exerting this influence

After completing these exercises, you should have an idea of what factors have had, and continue to have, a major influence on your thinking with regard to careers. These factors may be positive, negative, neutral, positive at one time and now negative, or vice versa.

They may be very "on the surface" of your thinking and a big part of your awareness about their influence on your career. It is also true that you may have uncovered influences that you had forgotten and were (or still are) surprised to recall events or people that have made real differences in your life. Just remember, the fact that these influences exist means they are a part of your thinking about this important issue. Therefore, you need to be aware of their potential influence. The messages that are conveyed from significant adults have a way of staying with a child into adulthood. Admonitions to girls such as, "Be a teacher so you'll have something to fall back on," or to boys, "You'll never be able to support a family on a musician's salary," often are recited later in life by adults as influential childhood messages heard again and again.

Exercise

The Meaning of "Career"

One of the most important aspects of a career "overhaul" is taking time to consider the meaning of "career." What does it mean to you? How would you define it? What values do you associate with it?

A career can be the most important part of a person's life or it can play a relatively minor role. How do you think about career in your life? Why is this important? Presumably, you are taking some time to think about your career as it currently exists. In order to accurately examine it, you need both a microscopic perspective and a macroscopic perspective. As you move along in future chapters of this book, you will find yourself examining your career from a very close point of view—what is your work day like, for instance. However, it is equally important for you to step way back and ask yourself, "What is this thing called work anyway, and what place does it hold in my life?" Even though we all use the terms "work," "career," and "job," it is also true that we mean many different things in our use of those terms. Clarifying what "career" means to you is a very important step. Just how big is career in your life? Just how much room do you want it to take up? Just what expectations do you have from it? And, what dreams does it need to fulfill? Take a few moments to answer the following questions. This exercise works best if you put down your initial "gut reaction" responses.

1) Define the meaning of the word "career."

_____

_____

_____

_____

2) What role does your career play in your life?

_____

_____

_____

_____

3) What role should your career play in your life?

_____

_____

_____

_____

4) What role do you want your career to play in your life?

_____

_____

_____

_____

The Career Fix-It Book

5

Exercise

Traditional versus Nontraditional

Answer the following questions, again putting down your first response.

1) The happiness one finds in a career is less important than the income derived from it.

   More True_____   Less True_____

2) A career is what you do from "9 to 5."

   More True_____   Less True_____

3) Being happy in a career is nice, but not necessarily of utmost importance.

   More True_____   Less True_____

4) Having a career is essential.

   More True_____   Less True_____

5) A career should not interfere with one's personal life and one's personal life should not interfere with one's career.

   More True_____   Less True_____

6) Work and play should be kept separate.

   More True_____   Less True_____

7) It is important to behave professionally while at work.

   More True_____   Less True_____

8) A career is about earning an income.

More True_____   Less True_____

9) Changing jobs often is a bad idea.

More True_____   Less True_____

10) To think that your career is what you make of it is being overly idealistic.

More True_____   Less True_____

Go back and take a look at your answers. Record here the number of "More True" and "Less True" answers.

MORE TRUE_____   LESS TRUE_____

The greater the number of "More True" responses, the more likely it is that you view the concept of career from a traditional point of view. This is not good or bad; it is simply something to be aware of about yourself. In viewing career from a traditional perspective, it is likely that you are deriving the income you want from it, that you are feeling that it is a respectable occupation, that it serves your family well. In viewing career from a more non-traditional perspective (a greater number of "Less True" answers), it is likely that you do not necessarily define yourself by your career, that you consider being happy in your career to be important, that your career and the rest of your life are likely to intermingle.

If you are unhappy in your career currently, it could be because you define work too traditionally and narrowly and could benefit by taking a more non-traditional look, or it could be that you are viewing work too non-traditionally and need to bring more traditional values into your thinking about work.

Chapter One Summary

On a scale of 1 to 5, with 1 representing "significant difficulty" and 5 representing "positive support," circle the number that best represents the influence of preconceived notions about your career.

1	2	3	4	5
Preconceived notions are contributing significantly to my career dissatisfaction.		Preconceived notions are a neutral influence on my career satisfaction.		Preconceived notions lend positive support to my career satisfaction.

Chapter Two

Choose a Career as You Would a Lover

"The future belongs to those who believe in the beauty of their dreams."
–Eleanor Roosevelt

Now that you have had a chance to examine some of your assumptions about the place of career in your life, let's go in the other direction. Let's throw out all of your "shoulds" and other outside influences about a career and get down to the basics of what you really like. As we have acknowledged, hidden influences can be important. Understanding what the term "career" means to you is important, and clarifying your own preferences is also a significant factor in determining your career happiness.

Why should this matter? Let's face it: how many of us go to the dentist because we want to? How many of us like to stand in line? Would we avoid these activities if we possibly could? Yes! Would we go to rather extreme lengths to avoid some things we don't like? Yes! Unfortunately, some of the things we don't like go with the job turf and can't be avoided if we want to do the fun things, too. But it pays to know what you like and don't like—actually, what you love and don't love. It is even possible to do something that is so pleasurable that if you do get paid for it—you think of that as a bonus. I have several friends who are artists. They love to paint. If they can sell a painting, so much the better. But they would rather live on the money from an occasional sale of a painting and get to paint each day than to have a regular job that would provide them with a stable income.

My first, and least favorite, job ever will help to illustrate my point about doing the things that you most love. I tend to be a pretty active person, and I like a lot of activity—mental and physical. I once had a job in high school that involved selling ladies hosiery in a department store. I had to wear high heels and stand on a hard marble floor behind a counter all day. The job was OK when there were customers. But when business was slow, I had to simply stand and look around, ready and willing to help whomever might wander by. This could involve a wait of an hour or more. I found myself desperate to escape the boredom, so I sought some entertainment: I watched the store detective. She was a middle-aged woman dressed as a shopper, and she would move around the store in a mysterious fashion. My greatest thrill was to see her catch someone, particularly if I had been observing the culprit. My second way of dealing with the monotony had to do with my two fifteen minute breaks and my half-hour lunch. I learned to get to the employees' lounge in two minutes on my break. I would read for eleven minutes and then take two minutes to rush back to my workstation. I did the same during my lunch "half hour." Reading had never been so precious to me, and I have never been so bored. I now know that inactivity is excruciating for me.

That same summer I had another job. This one involved turning on water hoses in people's yards in my neighborhood in Denver. City ordinances mandated that yards be watered very early in the morning, 5:00 A.M. to 7:00 A.M., in order to avoid the "rush hour" of people taking morning showers. Since most people did not want to get up and turn on their hoses so early, they would simply put the sprinkler out the night before, and I would make the rounds, returning two hours later to turn the hoses off. I'm sure this job would be considered "the worst" by many people, but it truly was enjoyable. I loved being active, being outside, being independent, getting to feel the crisp morning air, and doing something that was clearly of benefit, at least to the grass.

I'm sure that as you continue on through this chapter, you can point to your own versions of "ladies hosiery" and "lawn watering" jobs or activities.

Why is a job like a romantic relationship? Because it has to do with love. Why is it that in the area of romantic relationships, we are so willing to trust our feelings, but in other areas of our lives we tend to be more rational? When we fall in love we "know" that this person is right for us. We might be able to point out all the objectively wonderful qualities about the person, but those things hardly matter. What is important is how we feel about him/her, and this has little to do with objective qualities because this person touches something deep inside of us and gives us a feeling of connection or knowing. This is exactly the kind of connection that is important in career choice. The concept of falling in love with a job might sound ridiculous, but those people who are most happy in their careers are in love with what they do. The job brings out the best in these people. They are not bored; they love to go to work. All of us know certain things that we love to do, that inspire us, that bring us great satisfaction. But, so often, we fail to link these to our job choice. Choose your career as you would a life partner—go for what you love. Throw out the realistic aspects for the moment and dream.

So, get prepared to focus on what you "love" to do and what you "hate" to do. Chapter 1 concentrated on external influences and your past history of career thinking, this chapter will focus on present and future. If you find those old notions of, "It would be good for me," or, "My parents wanted me to do this," or, "My partner would never go along with this career," stop. You are thinking again. Rather, just go with the flow, and allow your imagination to take over during the exercises in this chapter. In other words, if an idea sounds good intellectually, it probably isn't.

You can retrieve any items from Chapter 1 that were fun and exciting to think about, but that's it.

Exercise

A Future Fantasy

This is a guided fantasy and requires the assistance of someone else. Or, if you have a tape recorder, you can tape the exercise and then play it back to yourself. The exercise takes about twenty minutes. Pick a quiet place where you can relax and not be interrupted. Sit back and either have your friend slowly read the exercise aloud or play your own tape of it. Allow your imagination to flow as you do this exercise.

Relax, get comfortable. Close your eyes. Take a few deep breaths. (Pause) Now, imagine that it is ten years from now. You are waking up in the morning in your own home or apartment. (Pause) You very slowly open your eyes and look around the room. (Pause) Take your time. (Pause) Note what the room looks like: What is the furniture like? What colors do you see? Are there windows? Does it seem that you are sharing this room with a partner? (Pause) As you think about your day ahead, consider how much you like your work. You feel energized by what you are doing in your career, but most of all, you find your work fun. (Pause) Now, slowly get out of bed, go to your closet, and decide what you will be wearing to work this day. Again, take your time. (Pause) While you are deciding, note what else might be in your closet. What types of clothes do you have? Are there other things in your closet such as sports equipment, hobby supplies, or perhaps children's things? (Pause) Pick out your clothes for the day and include shoes. Now, as you get dressed, imagine that you go into the other part of your living space in order to have some breakfast. You also gather your "work supplies" for the day. Lunch? Briefcase? Car keys? Tools? (Pause) Again, look around your living space and note the type of furniture, possible art on the walls, any signs of various interests and activities of those who live with you unless you are living alone. Are there any pets? Any children? (Pause) Notice the windows. Take a look outside and notice what you see. Are you in the country? Are you in a city? Are you in a warm or cold climate? Are you in an apartment or a house? Are you in a wooded area? In the mountains? At the seaside? (Pause) Make your final preparations for work and head out the door for your day's activities or, if you work at home, head for your work space there. (Pause) Note whether you drive to work, take a bus, or walk. How far away are you from work? Do you go by yourself? What do you see along the way? (Pause)

As you get close to your work setting, look around. What does the outside of your work environment look like? Is it a building? Is it a hospital or some sort of campus? Or possibly a construction site? Do you work indoors or out? (Pause) Slowly approach your work setting and go to the location where you do most of your work. (Pause) Take some time getting settled at your work place. Look around at your immediate environment. Are there others close to you or are you alone? What equipment do you use in your work: An architect's table? A telephone? A computer? A desk? Tools? (Pause) Now imagine that you begin your work. What do your do first? What are your overall responsibilities? (Pause) What do you like most about what you do? Take some time to imagine yourself going through the whole day of work. Just let your imagination go. Remember, the only consideration is that you enjoy what you do. (Longer Pause)

Now, gradually wrap up your work for the day and get ready to go home. (Pause) Say good-bye to any colleagues who may be there and head on out the door. (Pause) Tell yourself: I'm so lucky to be in a job that I like. (Pause) Slowly open your eyes.

Review your fantasy for a moment or two. Take a few moments to write down your fantasy. Do not edit it—report it exactly as you experienced it no matter how "corny" or unrealistic it may seem.

_____

_____

_____

_____

The Career Fix-It Book

_____

_____

_____

_____

_____

_____

_____

_____

_____

_____

_____

_____

This exercise helps you get in touch with your unconscious. Most of us are very much aware of our daily thoughts and base most of our decisions on them, but we don't often give ourselves opportunities to sit back, fantasize, and just let our imaginations wander. Unfortunately, much of who we are is not always available to our immediate conscious selves and is therefore lost to us—that knowledge may not be available when you approach a career decision from a strictly rational perspective. This exercise permits you to access some important information. Avoid judging yourself or your fantasy. Just let it be.

Let's switch gears for a moment. We are going to do another fantasy exercise, but this one is more present-oriented. It will give you some insights into the place work has in your life and also your feelings about your immediate job situation. Once again, I'm going to ask you to use your imagination. This time, you can do the exercise by yourself, but be sure to allow yourself enough time, privacy, and quiet to be able to complete it.

Exercise

Present Fantasy

(This assumes you are currently working. If not, skip to the end of the chapter.)

You have just been told that your employer is cutting back. The employer is "downsizing" and plans to lay off a number of employees. What is your initial reaction? Excitement? Disappointment? Relief? Fear? Now your employer tells you that you can choose to be among those employees who will receive an early buyout. The employer assures you that the terms are very generous and will allow you to retire early if you are getting close to retirement age or will provide you with six months of full pay to find a new job. You can opt to stay in your current position, and other than a few other employees leaving, your job will essentially remain unchanged. What do you decide? Why? As you contemplate the possibility of leaving your job, how do you feel? What are those things that give you a pang of regret? Those things that you realize you will miss after the initial excitement wears off? Those co-workers who you like? Get in touch with the potential feelings of relief: I won't ever have to do_____again! I won't ever have to see_____again! I can _____now just like I always wanted to do. Take your time with this exercise. Give it some serious thought. Make a decision either way and note how it makes you feel.

Now, write down your decision along with your reasons.

I plan to _____stay _____not stay in my job because:

_____

_____

_____

_____

_____

_____

_____

_____

_____

Things I would miss if I left:

_____

_____

_____

_____

_____

_____

_____

_____

_____

Things I would enjoy doing if I left:

_____

_____

_____

_____

_____

_____

_____

_____

_____

This exercise can give you some insight into how happy you are in your current work. It may be that there are aspects you like and others that you don't. By spelling these out, you can determine whether there are many reasons to leave and not many to stay, or whether your job is right for you, but requires a little tweaking to be better.

Exercise

A Sabbatical

Your boss tells you that you are going to be permitted to take a sabbatical. All employees need to upgrade their skills and will be provided an opportunity to do so. You will have a six-month leave of absence, and you get to pick what skills you want to polish! Take a few moments and decide how you would like to spend that six months. Recognize that you need to focus on improving your skills in your current job, but within those parameters there is a lot of room for choice. Would you like to improve something you currently do? Would you like to learn a new skill that would improve your current work? Would you choose a creative activity or perhaps a more manual skill? Be open to how you will spend this time. Your only goal is to find something that helps you in your current position to: 1) be of more use to your employer; and 2) provide you with greater job satisfaction.

My sabbatical:

_____

_____

_____

_____

_____

_____

The Career Fix-It Book

Chapter Two Summary

On a scale of 1 to 5, with 1 representing "significant difficulty" and 5 representing "positive support," circle the number that best represents the influence of emotional connection on your career.

1	2	3	4	5
Lack of emotional connection is contributing significantly to my career dissatisfaction.		Emotional connection is a neutral influence on my career satisfaction.		Emotional connection lends positive support to my career satisfaction.

**"To love what you do and feel that it matters—
how could anything be more fun."
—Katherine Graham**

Chapter Three

Stuck Doesn't Have to Be All Bad

"Only those who risk going too far can find out how far they can go."
—T.S. Eliot

You may have found after reading Chapters 1 and 2 that you and your work life are well suited and that you don't need to make any changes—or perhaps you need to do just a bit of fine-tuning. But chances are that if you are reading this book, you probably found that your work life isn't so great and that you do need to make some decisions, possibly major ones. Often, people who are unhappy in their jobs think that they need to totally change careers when, in actuality, minor alterations within their job will lead to significant satisfaction. Only you can determine whether you can make the adjustments you need within your current setting. The next few chapters are designed to help you determine whether you need a major overhaul or just a tune-up. Just remember, a tune-up is cheaper, so we will start with those sections (all chapters between 3 and 13 except 9), and if you find that these simply aren't enough, go for the larger change outlined in Chapter 9. Chapter 14 will pull together your "big picture."

Judy

Judy is a composite of a number of individuals I have seen over the years in my career counseling practice. Their presenting concern was always the same and the solution no different, so for that reason I'm depicting them as one person, "Judy." Judy has worked as a bookkeeper at home for fifteen years, raised a family, and has maintained a number of outside activities, mostly involving her family. Judy has enjoyed her bookkeeping job because it allows her considerable flexibility and pays sufficiently well to provide her with a good income. However, she always has wanted to work with people—specifically, in a counseling center helping college students with their concerns. (I always get a little threatened by people like Judy because it seems as though they are after my job.) She is sure this is the job for her. She has given it considerable thought. What does she have to do to get a job in this field? And, by the way, she only wants to work during the school year and no evenings or weekends. She is sure she would be very good at this type of work since she has helped her own children prepare for college. Judy did finish high school and three years of college, though most of her courses were in the field of business.

I always hate breaking the bad news to Judys. I try to ease in gently to get her to think a little more broadly—perhaps she might like to work as a counselor for individuals of all ages, or perhaps she might like to improve on her bookkeeping skills and work with a company as an accountant where she has more contact with people? No. She is sure about what she wants to do...period. Has she had an opportunity to research the career of college counselor or does she know any college counselors? No. I suggest that this might be a good place to start. But she is so certain of her idea, that she wants to get what she came in for: clear instructions on how to get hired as a college counselor. So, I have to be the bearer of bad news. I hate this part of my job, and I have yet to figure out how to work with Judys in a way that doesn't upset them.

First, I suggest to her that most college counselors have at least a master's degree in psychology or counseling. Many have doctorates, particularly those at four-year institutions, which is where she wants to work. She is surprised by this, but minimizes it as a "minor detail." Second, I tell her that these jobs are hard to get unless one is mobile and able to move to other states. She just laughs and tells me that is impossible since her husband is located here. Finally, I suggest to her that many of these jobs do involve summer time work and occasional evening and weekend hours. By this time, she is beginning to get upset; she seems to think I have something against her and am making this all up. All she wants is to find out how to get that job! I attempt to ease her irritation by suggesting that maybe she could take a few classes in psychology to check out her interests and to point her in the direction she wants to go. She leaves angry and convinced that I don't know anything about her new career or about how to counsel students.

Why did Judy become so frustrated? There are several reasons. First, Judy is living with a large number of misconceptions. (And you might want to check to see if you are, too.) She is under the impression that if she believes she is good at something, that career will open its doors to her instantly. Second, she is used to a style of work that allows for great flexibility. She would like to transfer this quality of her present work to a new career, and can't understand that this may not be possible. Moreover, she is unaware of what is involved in being trained for the particular occupation in which she is interested and knows nothing about the job market realities. Finally, she discounts her current skills, which could possibly be used to put together a new career for herself. But because Judy is determined to be a college counselor, she has automatically ruled out the possibilities of shaping her current training and skills into a career that satisfies at least some of her needs.

I only tell Judy's story because I have run into many individuals who think "Oh, wouldn't it be nice to be a _____," and then do nothing to learn about how realistic or unrealistic this plan is. One of the tricks of being happy in a career is to figure out a way to build on the skills you already have. It is possible to totally change careers in mid-life, but it requires tremendous sacrifice, typically in the time and finance areas. Therefore, I encourage you to start looking at your current situation and thinking about what you can do to improve it with the fewest possible changes.

OK, you are in a job that you don't like. The problem may be what you do, it may be who you work with, it may be where you work, or a combination of these. There are probably some things you like about the job. I'm going to suggest something radical—at least it was to me when I first heard it and tried it—mold your job to yourself! A mistake many of us make is to assume that we have to do the job that we were hired to do and cannot make any changes in it to our own liking. This is probably true for the first six months or a year. But after that time, you have more leverage than you may realize.

Stop for a moment and think about what Michaelangelo, or for that matter, any good sculptor, does when he works with a piece of marble. He was able to "see" the figure he was carving within the piece of marble. Therefore, his job was to cut out the unnecessary stone and keep the part that reflected what he was trying to create. He actively chipped off certain corners, refined certain grooves, sanded to smooth out the roughness. All of that activity was designed to "free up" the internal figure. In a sense, this is exactly what you may need to do with your job. If we assume for a moment that your job is that large piece of marble and that you are the sculptor, you need to picture the inside as your ideal job and figure out how to chip away at the extraneous "stuff" in your work in order to get to your own "work of art" within your career. And don't think for a minute that a job isn't a work of art: anyone who has had "peak moments" while working—those moments of intense satisfaction—knows just what I am talking about. Why not have more of those by more actively doing those things that allow for those moments of achievement and satisfaction?

Why is all this designing and molding necessary? Because even though we are often very active in designing the rest of our lives, for some reason we often think that we have no say over our job or job description. We pigeonhole ourselves into thinking that the job we have cannot change. For example, someone trained as an accountant may believe, "I was hired to be an accountant, so that is what I'll be as long as I am in this job." I once went to a workshop where the speaker talked about power in the work setting. He said that we, as employees, perceive the power to lie with the supervisor or boss. Ironically, the boss sees the power to lie with his or her boss, and that boss sees the power lying with the customer, a board, or someone else. What ends up happening, is that there is a certain amount of "power" that lies fallow or unclaimed. It is there for the taking. So I'm suggesting that you take it!

I was hired many years ago to be the career counseling coordinator in a university counseling center. The job involved much more career work than I had initially understood, and I also had a number of other interests that I wanted to pursue within my work setting. After a year on the job and successfully performing my responsibilities, I went to Mike Weissberg (my boss at the time and a very nice guy, luckily for me), and told him that I would like to shift my responsibilities to a broader range of duties. Specifically, I told him that I would like not to be the career coordinator anymore. He was a little miffed in the beginning because this meant that he had to do some shifting of personnel. But after a few weeks, he decided that I could go ahead and make the changes I had suggested. I picked up some of his duties that I enjoyed more than the career work, and he picked up some of the career work. I won't say he was thrilled by this, but we both knew that the changes would improve our work morale. Within a year, we had another opening on the staff, and Mike filled it with Dr. John Zaugra, a career specialist who is fantastic as a career counselor and does an outstanding job to this day of coordinating that same career program. I stayed with this agency for many years—in fact, I'm still there after twenty-five years! I'm sure I would be long gone had I not been able to shift my responsibilities from time to time.

I can hear some of you saying, "Yeah, sure, she had a nice boss who let her make the change." But let me say to you: don't forget the unclaimed power that exists in your work setting. Take the initiative to make changes in your job that will lead you to greater satisfaction. If you get a "no" for an answer, you really haven't lost anything. This is not to say that asking for a change or designing a new niche for yourself is necessarily easy. It isn't, and you may not achieve all that you want. But neither is quitting a job and moving on to a new one. Keep in mind that in most work settings you can mold your job to fit your own interests and keep yourself happy.

It is quite possible for you to do two things: 1) Ask your employer for some adjustments in your work, especially in the things with which you are unhappy.

It is surprising how often employers really don't mind and are willing to be accommodating. Especially if they think you are a good employee and want to keep you, they will tolerate some changes. The changes may be in your co-workers, your specific tasks, the hours you work, where you work, etc. 2) Make changes even within your own way of looking at your job. Start doing more of what you like and less of what you don't like. For example, delegate or trade filing or scheduling and focus on budgeting and account-keeping if you enjoy working more with numbers. It is quite likely that this step alone will get you to the point where your job is actually enjoyable. It will give you a greater feeling of appreciation from your employer, a sense of control in your life, and greater work satisfaction.

Anna

Anna received her degree in journalistic photography. She was looking for a career that would provide her with a satisfactory living as a single woman: one where the job market was good and which provided some variety and work outdoors. She took a position as a staff photographer for a mid-sized city daily newspaper, and at first took all of the assignments given to her. She enjoyed this and after a few years had worked her way up to a managerial position. She had assumed that "climbing the administrative ladder" was the thing to do, and she was probably slotted for head of the photo department. But she found that she did not particularly enjoy supervision and administration. Meanwhile, she had developed a strong interest in sports, particularly golf. After doing some serious soul-searching, she decided to step down from the administrative position and request more sports assignments. Her salary was unaffected since the administrative promotion had been considered minor. After her shift back to being a staff photographer, she began expressing her preferences for assignments. Since the other staff were aware of her fondness for golf, they were comfortable with her getting many of these assignments. She eventually gave up her plans to move to a bigger paper and began enjoying opportunities to expand her knowledge in sports and sports reporting.

Anna is a great example of someone who molded her job to her own liking. True, she was in this particular job for a number of years and had successfully established herself. True, she could afford to decline a promotion to a higher paying position. Some things are trade-offs in career decision-making. What is important to note about Anna is that she took charge of her career rather than allowing her employer to do so. Anna was, first of all, honest with herself about her own preferences at work. Second, she was assertive in expressing them to her employer. If she hadn't been both, she might have continued in a job that was less than satisfying for her. Or she might have moved to a new job that contained responsibilities that were less than enjoyable compared to sports photo assignments, and she might have been uprooted from her community of several years—one that she liked very much.

Go for as much training as you can. Get involved in your work setting. If your employer offers workshops and opportunities to learn new skills, do as much of that as you are allowed. If you receive money for school tuition, use it. If you are permitted to join professional organizations and participate in them, do it. Often, individuals are bored in their jobs, which is why they are unhappy. Receiving training in your current responsibilities, or learning new skills, can enliven even the most boring job. In addition, you typically will meet others with similar interests and can form new work relationships. We know that the college students who are happiest and tend not to drop out are those who get involved on campus. I believe that the same is true for the work environment.

Exercise

Mold the Job to Suit You

Make a list of what you like and do not like about your job (you might refer to the last chapter for this information).

Work Activities That I Most Like:

_____

_____

_____

_____

_____

_____

_____

_____

_____

_____

_____

_____

Work Activities That I Least Like:

_____

_____

_____

_____

_____

_____

_____

_____

_____

_____

B. From this list, circle the task that you most like and least like.

C. Write up a plan that would ease you out of the least-liked task and into the most-liked task. This is important to do because employers are busy people. If you simply go to them and say I don't want to do _____ anymore, they will probably say, "Fine," but not do much about it and probably will see you as a problem worker, not a team player. Having a plan in mind that you can present to the employer at the same time that you express your preferences makes the job much easier. If possible, the plan should be one that is feasible from the standpoint of other employees. In other words, it is highly unlikely that you will be able to trade jobs with someone else just because you would rather do his/her job. But it may be that you can shed a task that you dislike, or it may be that you are aware that a fellow employee would like to do more of what you dislike. Another factor to recognize is that the changes may not take place all at once. It took Anna a few years to mold her job to her satisfaction. Often just knowing that "it's in the works" makes the current situation tolerable.

The Career Fix-It Book

_____

_____

_____

_____

_____

_____

_____

_____

D. Find an opportune time to implement your plan. As noted above, this may occur over a period of time. You may want to talk with fellow employees to get a sense of their likes and dislikes. You may want to talk informally with your employer to feel out what might be possible. You may decide to make a formal request in writing to your employer, although most molding activities I've seen have come about in a more informal way. This is because you are going for what you want and yet not making major waves in the work setting. Most employers are very open to gradual, minor shifts, but become more suspicious of major requests. Work with your plan. Talk with close friends or family members to get their feedback on it. They can be supportive and help you with ideas for its implementation. It is up to you to get the plan rolling once you are comfortable with it. Be flexible. Remember that this is a form of "quiet rebellion," so you may need to take a little flak or readjust your goals somewhat, but the flak will go away in time and you will be on your way to doing what you most like to do at work.

Exercise

Get Trained

The following exercises will assist you in creating a more positive work environment for yourself.

1) Does your employer provide you with in-house training opportunities? If so, please list:

_____

_____

_____

_____

_____

_____

2) Do you have opportunities for training outside your place of employment (e.g., tuition reimbursement, workshops, conferences, community education)? If so, please list:

_____

_____

_____

_____

_____

_____

Go back and star those activities that you plan to take advantage of in the next year. In the space below, explore how the items you starred can help improve the work environment for you.

_____

_____

_____

_____

_____

_____

_____

Chapter Three Summary

On a scale of 1 to 5, with 1 representing "significant difficulty" and 5 representing "positive support," circle the number that best represents the influence of your job responsibilities on your career.

1	2	3	4	5
Dislike of my job responsibilities is contributing significantly to my career dissatisfaction.		My job responsibilities are a neutral influence on my career satisfaction.		My job responsibilities lend positive support to my career satisfaction.

"If you really want something, you can figure out how to make it happen."
—Cher

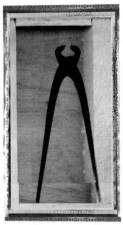

Chapter Four

And You Thought It Was About the Job Itself

"I will permit no man to degrade my soul by making me hate him."
—Booker T. Washington

You have read the first few chapters of this book, but haven't yet hit on the source of your unhappiness? If your problems at work are not related to your actual job responsibilities, then it's probable that your difficulties come from one of these three areas: 1) your co-workers, 2) your work environment, or 3) your transition between home and work.

Your Co-Workers

Let's tackle the people part now. This is a difficult subject because, as we all know, it is hard—if not impossible—to change others. You can, however, arrange to be around the people you don't like, or those who pull you down, as little as possible. Remember, you can "mold" your job to some extent. That includes with whom you associate.

Positive relationships are a key to happiness, whether at home or at work. I'm sure that we have all had the unpleasant experience of having a dispute with someone we live with. Unless resolved rather quickly, it can "eat away" at us. My mother always told me not to go to bed mad. It was pretty good advice, but advice that I haven't always followed. I've spent more than a few nights tossing and turning trying to sort out a dispute that I was having with someone I'm close to. It feels lousy to be out of sorts with someone we love.

Disputes among neighbors are another source of interpersonal tension that can cause significant strain. I recently purchased a beautiful little cottage on a lake. It was a quaint A-frame nestled among tall pine trees with a large deck overlooking a serene lake. Ah, the perfect place to get away and feel no stress or tension. Wrong. As soon as I had purchased the cottage and furnished it with cozy overstuffed chairs and reading lamps, my neighbor on the lake decided to build an addition to his house. My irritation that the addition came within a foot of my property line and that there were bulldozers and electric hammers going throughout the summer was only exacerbated by his noisy dog who came tromping across to my property to relieve himself daily. So much for bliss.

My point is that the best of "settings," be they home, vacation, or work, can be spoiled by tension between you and someone else. Therefore, I would encourage you to remove yourself, when possible, from people that cause you stress and strain. In the case of the cottage, I liked the setting enough that I did not want to sell it. So I lived through the noise of the addition, and, fortunately, it was completed quickly. I put in some shrubbery along the property line that served as both a visual and literal boundary marker for animals and people. If you are serving on committees or working on a project with people you don't like, aim at shifting to other projects. If your break time is the same as theirs, change your schedule accordingly.

Perhaps someone with whom you are having ongoing competition or an "I'm right, you're wrong" battle is making the workplace miserable for you. Let it go. I know, you think it's too important to drop. But maybe your mental health is too important to continue the fight. Weigh what you would gain by letting go of your negative feelings against what you gain by maintaining them. I'm willing to bet that you soon will realize that an engagement with a negative person/situation on a continuing basis is a tremendous drag on your energy. Try looking for this person's good points. Everyone has at least one. Focus on that and stop dwelling on what bothers you about the person.

Marie

Marie is on the faculty at a small college. In department meetings, she began noticing that one group tended to bond together and veto many of the new ideas that came up. These individuals seemed to have a negative attitude and were not particularly friendly to others on the faculty. Marie found herself often challenging this group in departmental meetings because she did not agree with much of what they said. She felt it was important that she be able to share her opinions. In addition, it irritated her that this group was causing some roadblocks to departmental business. She saw their actions as an ethical issue and was determined to stop what she perceived as unprofessional behavior.

While other faculty were irritated by the group, they did not "take on" these individuals directly as often as Marie did. The atmosphere in the department grew increasingly hostile, and Marie found that "the group" was blaming her for a number of recent troubling occurrences. This only angered Marie more. She determined to fight the group because it seemed like "the right thing to do" in the name of the department. Unfortunately, the group was just as determined, and therefore they began making life for Marie a real hell.

It finally became clear to Marie that she could not "win" with this group. Her dedication to the department and her desire for it to function in the best ways were admirable, but they were also causing her to be the target of significant hostility. She recognized that the battles with this group were dominating her work life and taking away from what she really enjoyed most, her teaching. She was able to let go, stop challenging the group in meetings, shift her work activities so that she was not on committees with the same people and re-focus on her teaching. The group is still there and is still causing problems in the department, but Marie is once again happy in her job and feels that engaging in "no win" situations are not profitable for her. She can turn over the troubles of the department to others.

In some ways, what Marie did was she "lost her ego." She gave up having to be "right," having to make sure that her ideas were implemented, and getting the department to function in appropriate ways. She had to drop what, in effect, had become her "causes." We often get very attached to ideas about work, values in the way things are done, and we want to see our ideas win out. They are probably very good ideas! But by becoming so attached to them that they overshadow our happiness in our work, we may find that they are not worth it. It becomes necessary to give up your ego, let your causes go, and focus on the parts of your job you enjoy.

Your Work Environment

A pleasant work environment is very important to your happiness. There are many things that affect how we feel. The color of the walls, the temperature in the workplace, the comfort of the furniture, or even the quality of the coffee can make a difference. And that is to name just a few of the things that influence our everyday happiness. Even more important than the "ambiance" of the work environment are the invisible surroundings. Is the mood of the office enjoyable? A recent study showed that employers were providing "fun" activities at work in order to recruit better employees. They found that when they offered an "everyone gets along," fun work setting, people wanted to come to work for them.

During my one-year internship for my doctoral degree, I was under considerable stress to prove myself in order to complete my Ph.D. I had to pass my internship, which meant being constantly evaluated, in terms of both the amount and the quality of my work. I also had to complete a dissertation. There were three other interns going through the same thing with me. Oddly enough, one of the main things that made that year not only tolerable but also almost fun was the fact that we played bridge every lunch hour. We all looked forward to that one hour during the day when we came together, had fun with a challenging card game, laughed, and relaxed.

If you can be in an enjoyable work environment, you can tolerate a lot of other things, including less pay, tasks that you don't always like, and longer hours. A positive work environment is one of those things that if we are reminded of it, we know we want it. But we don't always think about including that as a major criterion in our job searches. Even if your current work environment is not fun, you can do some things to improve it. Create some activities: monthly potlucks, pools on sports events, funny cartoons and jokes, contests, an exercise club, an annual "awards" banquet based on people's funny mistakes during the year. These typically are inexpensive activities and provide a major boost to the staff. They also detract from negative emotions.

MC

MC is a guy who likes humor. In fact, he kind of specializes in it. In his work setting, he often passes cartoons and jokes around. He does this with a tremendous degree of sensitivity. He doesn't make sexist or racist jokes or jokes about any of the employees in the setting. In addition, because he is good with humor, he is selective about the type of humor he passes around—only the really funny jokes. This practice has helped the morale in his office tremendously, not only because the jokes are amusing, but also because there is a sense that MC does this out of caring for others. He started including little heartwarming stories as well as the cartoons and jokes. He had Chicken Soup for the Soul stories long before that book was published. I came to know about MC because he began putting some of his jokes and stories on a computer listserve that I share with him and several others. Every so often (he particularly likes doing this on Fridays), he passes on one of his stories. I always feel a little twinge of happiness when I see his name on my computer. It means I am going to be treated to a great joke or story. Many of us on the listserve have commented on how much we appreciate MC's little additions. They give us a boost often on a day where everything is going wrong at work. They also remind me that there is a lot of power in one little gesture of goodwill.

Exercise

Create a Positive Environment

1) Who/what is the problem? What person do you have the most difficulty with in your work environment? If you like all of the people, skip to the next exercise.

_____

How often do you interact with this person?

_____

_____

_____

_____

Would it be possible for you to interact less with this person without causing yourself more grief? How?

_____

_____

_____

_____

_____

2) Who do you like best in your work environment?

_____

Why?_____

_____

_____

How often do you interact with this person?

_____

_____

_____

Would it be possible for you to interact more with this person? How?

_____

_____

_____

_____

Exercise

Improving Morale

Make a short list of "fun" activities that would be easy to implement at work and that would improve the workplace morale.

1.

2.

3.

4.

5.

Are there other employees that you might get to help you with the fun activities? Who?

1.

2.

3.

Use the information you learned about your work environment in the above exercises to make some positive changes in it.

Transition Between Home and Work

Most of us define work as the time we actually spend at work. Our clock starts ticking when we enter the door or punch the time card. In fact, work overlaps significantly with our personal lives. We may take papers, reports, etc., home with us on a regular basis. And even if we are not doing actual work, we are probably thinking about some aspect of our jobs during our off hours. Hopefully, these are positive thoughts! But often they aren't. As a psychologist, I've had people say to me frequently: "How do you do it? I'd be taking all those people's problems home with me every night." In fact, I used to. Most of us cannot make a clear-cut break between work and home. It makes sense that we would think about work to some degree during our off-work time. We may even think that we are doing something very positive for our work setting by thinking about work at home. Perhaps some of our best problem solving occurs when we are mulling over ideas while we shower. This can be taken too far, however. I once had a colleague who insisted on coming to work a half hour late. He said that he was "thinking about work" on his way to work and therefore that was part of his workday. He didn't last long in the job, but you get the point. We may even socialize with some of our work friends, thereby blending work and home even more.

Because you are looking for ways to improve your life as it relates to work, you might find it helpful to think a little about the way work enters your personal life. Is this "intrusion" negative, positive, or both?

If you find yourself thinking about work more than you want to (for some people, it may be helpful or necessary to think about work at home), you might try doing a little damage control. Consider how much time you want to spend at home doing work or thinking or talking about your job at home. If this feels like an issue for you, you may consciously want to minimize that time. Most likely, by just focusing on spending less time on it, you will. But if you find yourself thinking about it even when you don't want to, try the following exercise.

Exercise

Work Worry Time

Set aside a specific amount of time (between fifteen and thirty minutes) at home to focus on work. During that time, do nothing but think about work. Don't eat, don't read, don't exercise, don't talk to others, and don't watch TV. Just think about work (or do work). The rest of your time at home you can do all of those other things. And when intrusive thoughts about work enter your mind, just say to yourself, "I'll think about it during my work worry time." Then let it go.

The transition time from home to work also can be used effectively for helping to reduce the effects of a negative work environment. Most of us have up to an hour in transition. We frequently use this time to daydream, think about home, think about work, eat, etc. Generally, we don't structure driving time. It just happens. Too often, many of us who drive in traffic arrive at work already very stressed. The tailgaters are out in full force. And the commute home usually isn't any better.

Use your transportation/transition time more purposefully. For instance, if you really need to take work home, you may be able to find a way to use your travel time for this. As much as I don't like drivers who are busier talking on their cell phones than watching traffic, this "commute calling" is a way to accomplish some tasks en route. The same goes for using a tape recorder in your car to get ideas down. That way, you can do less work when you get home. However, this idea is only for those who label themselves workaholics.

What I really recommend in terms of the transition from home to work is some down time. Use this golden time to do things that are fun. It is particularly helpful to have this time to yourself if you work with people non-stop and go home to a house full of people. It may be the only time you have to yourself all day. Use it for pleasant thoughts or images versus worrisome thinking or anger at traffic. Use it for relaxation and stress reduction. There are a variety of ways to do this, but my favorite is to listen to books on tape. Some of the best books I have ever "read" are those I've checked out from the audio section at my local library. My favorites are novels, but I've also enjoyed self-help tapes. Books on tape provide a great distraction from heavy traffic, rude drivers, and bad weather. Since you are caught up in the book, these things are not as irritating. A friend of mine was sure that the time it took her to get to work was too short to listen to books. So she resisted trying it out for a long time. Finally, she did and can't believe how much she enjoys it. Even ten minute rides are sufficient for books on tape.

Some people drink coffee in their cars, and that makes the journey more tolerable. Although I might not recommend coffee since it is a stimulant, having something healthy to drink also can be helpful in making the trip less stressful. And you can always try music. If the stress of traffic gets to you, use soothing music and turn it up. Keep the inside of your car clean. A trashy car is yet another stress-producing thing and it makes feeling comfortable and relaxed much more difficult.

Exercise

Transition Time

I use the time between work and home

☐ positively

☐ negatively

☐ unsure

While I am in transit, I typically

☐ worry

☐ get angry

☐ day dream

☐ think about work

☐ think about home

☐ relax

When I am at home, I think about work

☐ most of the time

☐ some of the time

☐ not at all

When I think about work, it is in

☐ positive, energizing ways

☐ stress-causing ways

☐ both

Exercise

Smooth Transition

In order to add a more peaceful transition between my work and home life, I plan to:

_____

_____

_____

_____

_____

_____

_____

_____

_____

_____

_____

_____

Chapter Four Summary

On a scale of 1 to 5, with 1 representing "significant difficulty" and 5 representing "positive support," circle the number that best represents the influence of your work environment on your career.

1	2	3	4	5
My work environment is contributing significantly to my career dissatisfaction.		My work environment is a neutral influence on my career satisfaction.		My work environment lends positive support to my career satisfaction.

"Work, the object of which to serve one's self is the lowest. Work, the object of which is merely to serve one's family is the next lowest. Work, the object of which is to serve more and more people, in widening range...is social service in the fullest sense, and the highest form of service we can reach."
—Charlotte Perkins Gilman

Chapter Five

If You're Not Having Fun, Lower Your Standards

"The trouble with the rat race is that even if you win, you're still a rat."
—Lily Tomlin

Only you know how much work-related stress you are under—you and those closest to you, that is. If you find yourself skipping breaks, lunch hours, coming in early, or leaving work late routinely, you are probably working too hard. If you would rather work than do "fun stuff" such as going to movies, reading books for pleasure, and engaging in hobbies, you are probably working too hard. Some of us can "take it." We like the high that we get from being addicted to work. However, there is always a fine line even with Type A personalities that determines how fun work really is. Type As can get burned out, just like everyone else. You may have set the standard of perfection for yourself and therefore you may be very hard on yourself about your work. As your own worst critic, you look for what is wrong rather than what is right about your performance. Small mistakes throw you. Both of these characteristics—working too much and being overly self-critical—can cause dissatisfaction in your work. Not only that, but these same habits frequently extend into your personal life, and you are therefore probably doing the same stress-causing behaviors at home.

Both excessive work and self-criticism come from the same source—a desire to be recognized and cared about. This is a good thing to want, but without recognizing how subtly it controls us, we can get into big trouble. In our culture, accomplishment, recognition, and others' respect are signs of being successful in our work. Unfortunately, they do not automatically equal happiness, even though most of us make that assumption. In fact, these external signs often lead to more work! Once I wrote a grant for a very worthwhile community project. It was outside my usual job responsibilities, so it was an added burden. The grant was awarded and the project was a success. Of course, I had to work doubly hard to complete the grant and do my job. That was all right since the project was short-lived. However, suddenly I had become the in-house expert on writing grants. My boss wanted me to write another grant. Co-workers were referred to me to ask for assistance in writing grants. All of this on top of my regular job. Sound familiar? If so, you are equating success with happiness and defining success by quantity of work accomplished. Workaholics often discount the other rewarding aspects of work. Such pleasures as coffee breaks with co-workers, occasionally leaving a little early to go shopping, or going for a walk in the middle of the day can make work much more satisfying. And saying no to an extra project can feel very good if you develop the right attitude.

Why is it important to keep your workload reasonable? For several reasons. First, we live in a competitive culture with a strong work ethic. When is the last time you heard your boss (or for that matter, even yourself) say, "Hey, why don't you take an extra day of vacation." Are you aware that Europeans typically have six weeks of vacation a year? Many European cities practically shut down in August because so many Europeans have that month off work! That notion is alien to most of us. If we are lucky, we get three weeks of vacation a year. Since our mindset is one of "work hard" as the norm, those of us who have an extra dose of guilt or competitive desire work even harder. Because the bar is set high already, we don't realize that we may be spending way too much of our lives caught up in our job and also don't recognize the symptoms of work "burn-out."

Overworking does two things: first, it consumes too much of your waking hours and does not leave enough time for other interests, relationships, and the fun stuff of life. Second, it creates a kind of numbness—because you are so caught up in the work, you actually lose your ability to be aware of and discern the warning signs of overwork. Sounds ironic. But as is true with many unhealthy habits, we are so numbed by the behavior that we cease to realize what we're doing. There are many examples of this in our personal lives: addictions such as gambling, overeating, and alcoholism often start out as seemingly harmless activities but progress into self-destructive habits. The warning signs are often there in the beginning, but disappear as the behavior gets more consuming. You have probably heard of the term "denial" applied to various kinds of addictions. Therein lies the danger of excessiveness in any behavior. We know on some level that things are not right in our lives, but we become blind to its dangers. If this is you in relation to excessive work habits, it is time to step back and reclaim your awareness. Very likely your work habits are the main contributors to your unhappiness.

I rode in the RAGBRAI (the Registers Annual Great Bike Ride Across Iowa) a few years ago. There were ten thousand of us riding our bikes from the west border of Iowa to the east. Each day we had a certain distance to cover. Some riders started off at 5:00 A.M. and arrived at their next destination three hours later. Others of us took most of the day to get there (not because I didn't want to get there—it just took me that long!). At first, I was hard on myself for not being able to go faster. I hated all those bikers who sped past me. The first couple of days were pretty miserable for this reason. And then, I saw it! A big red school bus which was the accompanying transportation for some bikers. Painted in huge letters on the side of the bus was the following, "IF YOU'RE NOT HAVING FUN, LOWER YOUR STANDARDS!" I decided to lower my standards then and there, and the rest of RAGBRAI was a lot more fun for me. (I did finish by the way. I took a photo of that bus, and eight years later I still have it in a frame on my desk—just a reminder when I get carried away with myself.)

Alice

Alice is a dynamic, bright woman who is high up in the marketing office of a very large, well-known international corporation. Her job is obviously a "big deal," and she makes good money and enjoys the prestige that goes with the position. But more than anything else, she likes to accomplish things. She gets up every morning at 4:00 A.M. and works for two hours at home. She then goes to the office and has an extremely hectic schedule. She typically goes home around 4:00 in the afternoon and "takes it easy" for a few hours before going to bed. Taking it easy usually means making some phone calls, playing with her cat, sitting and smoking cigarettes (two packs a day), and watching TV. She lives alone. I met Alice in a social situation and we became friends. When I asked her what she likes to do, she was somewhat at a loss. She had no hobbies to speak of, she was relatively introverted so did not socialize a whole lot. She didn't like going to movies or cultural activities, and she didn't travel for pleasure. The few activities that she could identify included those noted above and reading true crime books. I think she never paused long enough to bother to develop some interests. When she did try to do things with friends, it was as if she didn't know how. Her few pleasurable activities were so important to her that she could not conceive of quitting smoking, and she became extremely distraught when her cat became sick once. Most recently, she negotiated for a buy-out, early retirement from the corporation. She was very excited at the prospect. Her boss agreed, but the last I heard he had talked her into keeping the buy-out money and still working three days a week for him. My hunch is that those three days will soon be five or six.

A friend of mine recently told me that being too busy is a form of violence. I think she is right. If you wonder whether you are a "workaholic" and using work in ways that are ultimately unhealthy for you, here is a short exercise that may provide you with an answer.

Exercise

Am I a Workaholic?

1) I evaluate self and work in quantity accomplished.

    Yes_____   No_____   Unsure_____

2) I take on work because I believe I can do it better than others.

    Yes_____   No_____   Unsure_____

3) I am reluctant to take a vacation.

    Yes_____   No_____   Unsure_____

4) I am secretly critical of others who do not work as hard as I do.

    Yes_____   No_____   Unsure_____

5) I ignore emotions that suggest a problem, e.g., anger, sadness, etc.

    Yes_____   No_____   Unsure_____

6) I try to read quickly.

    Yes_____   No_____   Unsure_____

7) I schedule all of my time, allowing for little free time.

    Yes_____   No_____   Unsure_____

8) I get irritated at slow traffic.

    Yes_____   No_____   Unsure_____

9) I hardly notice an increase in smoking, drinking, or use of medications.

    Yes_____   No_____   Unsure_____

10) I rarely do nothing.

     Yes_____   No_____   Unsure_____

11) I eat rapidly.

     Yes_____   No_____   Unsure_____

12) I always try to do more than one thing simultaneously.

     Yes_____   No_____   Unsure_____

     TOTAL:

     "Yes" Answers_____ "No" Answers_____ "Unsure" Answers_____

If you answered "yes" more than six times, dissatisfaction in your work may be related to workaholism. If that is the case, exercise 2 has some suggestions for dealing with this problem. This is one of the harder work problems to solve; therefore if you see no improvement in this area, you might consider seeing a professional counselor for a few sessions focused on reducing your addiction to work.

Exercise

Ways to "Get Over It"—Work That Is

Check items that most appeal to you.

- ☐ "Schedule" free time.

- ☐ Leave some things uncompleted.

- ☐ Stop counting everything.

- ☐ Sit back and let others volunteer.

- ☐ Look for meaning in your relationships rather than in your work.

- ☐ Add more esthetic experiences in your life: flowers, music, garden walks.

- ☐ Exercise moderately, not competitively.

- ☐ Spend time with your favorite friend.

- ☐ Stop and take a few deep breaths.

- ☐ Count your blessings.

- ☐ Be prepared for some mild criticism about how you are not working as hard as usual.

- ☐ Think about how you would spend your time if you had only six months to live—and then live it that way.

☐ Include some form of spirituality or wonder at nature in your life on a regular basis.

Chapter Five Summary

On a scale of 1 to 5, with 1 representing "significant difficulty" and 5 representing "positive support," circle the number that best represents the influence of workaholism on your career.

1	2	3	4	5
Workaholism is contributing significantly to my career dissatisfaction.		Workaholism is a neutral influence on my career satisfaction.		Workaholism lends positive support to my career satisfaction.

"You can get lonesome—being that busy."
—Isabel Lennart

Chapter Six

Moving—It's More Than Renting a U-Haul

"We didn't have much, but we sure had plenty."
–Sherry Thomas

Career is associated with promotion and—in our competitive culture—success. This often involves a geographic move. As a psychologist, I have met with many clients who could not understand why they felt so unhappy after a promotion and requisite move. They felt as though they should be delighted with their success. However, they felt lonely, they reported marital problems, their spouses had difficulty finding employment in the new location, or if they had moved alone, they often reported difficulty in making new friends and sadness about leaving old friends. Getting children enrolled in new schools, helping them to make new friends, finding a new dentist, getting all the addresses changed, dealing with movers, saying goodbye to what are sometimes lifetime friends created significant stress in my clients' lives—all at a time when they were supposed to be happy about their successful career development. Having made a couple of professional moves myself, I understand some of these feelings.

Although there may be considerable value in staying in one location, this is often overlooked in job move considerations. Why is it that we do not realize the value of staying put? Part of it has to do with our belief in the value of independence. Just think about the American injunction to, "Go West, young man." The whole notion of being singularly strong, courageous, free, and adventuresome has been woven into the American persona since the country was founded. Freedom and independence are cornerstones of our country. Therefore, it makes sense that these values would affect our view of individual freedom in all areas of our lives. We prize our ability to travel, move at a moment's notice, and take advantage of opportunity. Individualism is valued over community and group relations. Because of our collective heritage, we often do not think about the sacrifices involved in achieving individual freedom. Even our notions of child rearing support the ultimate goal of independence. In traditional theories of Western psychology, the notion of individual development has long been held as the ultimate goal for the child becoming an adult. We encourage our children from a very early age to crawl, walk, talk, do well in school, participate in sports, go to the best college, and become financially independent. Failure at any of the various milestones of individual development is considered very serious, and dependency is considered a "no-no." Boys who are too close to their mothers may be called sissies. Fathers who make choices to take paternity leave when their wives give birth are still in the minority. Children over twenty-five years old still living with their parents are thought of in our mainstream culture as odd.

As a result of the ingrained values of becoming independent and moving on to new opportunities, we often downplay the value of staying in one location, putting down roots, and becoming "interdependent" with the individuals in our extended family and community.

When I made a move for professional reasons a number of years ago, I simply never made the adjustment to the new place. I had decided that I needed a new career experience. I had worked for six years as a psychologist in a college counseling center in the Midwest. The job was quite satisfying; however, I had bought into the American notion of moving to a new place as fun and adventure—especially having moved to the Northwest. How could anyone not want to live in the Seattle area? A few friends had moved there in the previous year and were enjoying it, so I decided to join them. I accepted a job very similar to my current position at the time—a psychologist in a college counseling center in Tacoma—packed up the furniture and headed West with my nine-year-old daughter. We rented a waterfront-furnished cottage on Vashon Island, a picturesque place with a view of Mt. Rainier, just a fifteen-minute ferry ride from Seattle or Tacoma. What could be more ideal? I enrolled my daughter in the local island school and the usual music lessons and horsebackriding, which was her love. She actually adapted pretty quickly, but I didn't. I couldn't understand why I was unhappy. I was living in one of the most beautiful places in the world, I had a good job, and I had a few friends in the area. What was wrong? I convinced myself that it was just a matter of time, that I would adjust. I kept telling myself, as I have told several of my clients, "The first six months of a move are always the hardest." However, by the end of a year, things were no better. I was seriously depressed. After a trip back to the Midwest to visit friends, I realized that I was missing my old friends (the ones I had known for many years and with whom I had a history) and the Midwest—hard as that may be to believe. I was so happy to see those cornfields! I decided to move back to the Midwest, a decision that I have never regretted. It just felt right to be there.

Prior to my move to the Northwest, I had no idea that landscape, or the feeling of the air of a place, or the change in seasons could make such a difference in my "feeling at home." Now, I visit the Northwest often since my daughter, who is now an adult, went to college and has married and settled down there. And each time I go, I am happy to visit and glad to return "home."

For some reason, in our culture the emotional impact of career moves has not been considered; relocating is, in fact, taken for granted as part of what one does to advance professionally. However, being uprooted can result in years of feelings of disconnectedness and loss of personal history. People say it takes a full year to get used to a new place. I say it takes at least that, and often there is lasting emotional damage.

When I was entering the seventh grade, my father accepted a position in Denver, Colorado. We had been living in a small town in Missouri (my parents' hometown). While I made the transition pretty well, my high school–aged brother fared far worse. He went from a small-town high school where he knew everyone to a large city high school where he knew no one and where friendships were solidly formed by the time students reached their sophomore year. I remember him trying to figure out how to fit in. He tried joining the ROTC, which he later found out was made up of the "nerds" of the school. He tried wearing white bucks (this was in 1957), and that helped to some extent. But he never really "made it" at East High School, a very competitive place, either academically or socially. He had difficulty transferring his small-town Missouri identity to such a place. He was an average student and stayed out of trouble. But he was not happy. He was lonely, and he longed for his fishing buddies in the small Missouri town. Not until he adopted the culture of Colorado by becoming an outstanding downhill skier and went on to college at the University of Colorado did he begin to enjoy meaningful friendships once again—several years after we had moved.

Career moves are all too often separated from the more emotional, family side of life. Fortunately, more is being written about individuals who have decided to pass up a promotion because it means moving to a new place. But for the most part, this area of career planning is rarely discussed. The sadness that comes from friendships ending—for both children and adults—is underestimated or not even addressed. And moves are hard not only on those who leave but on those left behind. Often, elderly parents or adult siblings are left; children lose their aunts and uncles who can provide care and mentoring. We wonder why there is so much depression. It is increasing at an alarming rate and the average age for the onset of depression is decreasing rapidly. The reasons cited are often the lack of connectedness and significant meaningful relationships with others. This may be the single most important factor in an individual's and family's happiness, but it is disregarded when career moves are considered.

For this reason, seriously examine a decision to make a geographic career move. Factor in the emotional impact the move will have. Is it worth it? Sometimes, staying put can be very rewarding. Turning down a promotion and more money may mean several years of family happiness (and possibly saved marriages, saved money for the cost of a move, saved hours of therapy, saved medical expenses). Even putting up with a job that is not quite as great as you would like may be better than going for a new job that brings with it a significant degree of uncertainty. Remember, you can mold your present job to some extent more easily than you can a brand new job. At least try that first.

Of course, when you are unhappy in a job, you feel as though everything is terrible, and your tendency might be to leave. However, you may be throwing out the baby with the bath water. The job difficulty has become magnified and therefore the prospect of leaving is magnified—it feels like a solution to all your problems. It isn't. There are difficulties in any job. I suggest that you try everything, including waiting for a period of time (sometimes the difficulty goes away), before leaving. Talk to friends and family before making a job change. Consider all aspects of your life before deciding to uproot it. Then, if your work situation is still that bad, go ahead and look for something new. However, I would encourage you to look close to where you currently are, possibly even within the same company or agency or within the same or a nearby community.

Exercise

Your Connections

How invested are you in your current setting?

Make a list of your ten closest friends and place a check next to those who live within a twenty-five mile radius of you.

1)_____ ☐

2)_____ ☐

3)_____ ☐

4)_____ ☐

5)_____ ☐

6)_____ ☐

7)_____ ☐

8)_____ ☐

9)_____ ☐

10)_____ ☐

List the ten family members you feel closest to and indicate how many of them live within a twenty-five mile radius.

1)_____ ☐

2)_____ ☐

3)_____ ☐

4)_____ ☐

5)_____ ☐

6)_____ ☐

7)_____ ☐

8)_____ ☐

9)_____ ☐

10)_____ ☐

List organizations, volunteer work, or community activities in which you are involved.

1.

2.

3.

4.

5.

If you have an immediate family, do a similar activity for each member of your family. Or, have family member(s) fill out this section. After all, someone else's perceptions may be quite different from your own.

Family member(s):

Closest friends:

The Career Fix-It Book

Closest relatives:

Community involvement:

If you find that you and/or your family are very connected in your local community, you may want to consider what you will lose by a move. If you and/or your family are not particularly connected, you have less to lose. If you are more connected in a different community, you may want to consider relocating there. As you contemplate a move to a new community, you might also research it to determine whether connectedness is possible there. For example, are there similar organizations, opportunities, and social events?

Chapter Six Summary

On a scale of 1 to 5, with 1 representing "significant difficulty" and 5 representing "positive support," circle the number that best represents the influence of geographical location on your career.

1	2	3	4	5
My geographical location contributes significantly to my career dissatisfaction.		My geographical location is a neutral influence on my career satisfaction.		My geographical location lends positive support to my career satisfaction.

"If I don't have friends, then I ain't got nothin'."
—Billie Holiday

Chapter Seven

Save for a Sunny Day

**"Civilization is a limitless multiplication of unnecessary necessities."
–Mark Twain**

If you stop and think about it, a good portion of your problems, both at work and at home, can come from money. Either you have big bills that need to be paid or you want things that you don't have the money to buy. It may also be true that you have an ideal standard of living that you must achieve or maintain, and the money just doesn't quite stretch. These money-related problems take a variety of forms. Obviously, having large credit card debt feels like an albatross around your neck. It causes daily worry, excessive interest payments, and adds to the feeling that you have to make more money. The same is true for a large home mortgage or car payment that stretches your income to the breaking point. By the time you make the mortgage, you have next to nothing left of your paycheck.

The obvious impact of these financial concerns is evident: you worry, you try to budget, you get irritated if others in your family spend money, you go deeper in debt, and the cycle continues. But, the more serious result of this kind of trouble is not as obvious: its subtle influence on your career choices. Having large debt or insufficient income to support your standard of living is not much different than a prison sentence. And it begins to feel just like that. If you are seriously in debt, you are locked into having to make a certain amount of money. Period. There is no choice. You may have to stay on in a job that you don't like in order to bring in the necessary income. You may not be able to take six months or a year off in order to go to school or try some new type of career. You are certainly unable just to quit your job and do nothing for awhile. Since you don't have a lot of options, you don't think about possibilities. This constricts your opportunities to get into more satisfying work or career activities. How many of us know people, or even ourselves, who have thought or said, "I wish I could just go be a beach bum for six months." We mean it! But it is also true that what is really bothering us is the lack of freedom from the obligation of financial responsibility.

I have sworn off credit cards many times. I cut them up and pay them off only to get a couple of new ones in the mail, and bingo, the balance begins to rise again. I think to myself, "I'll use this one only for airline trips, so I can get the free miles." Or "I'll put my holiday presents on this one and pay the full balance at the end of January." Who do I think I'm kidding? It is frightening how easy it is these days to borrow money. We get lulled into an expectation about our standard of living—a standard based in the lifestyles depicted in magazine ads, and which would require an annual income of $200,000 to maintain.

I get very concerned about the students at my university. Hardly a day goes by without credit card company reps setting up in our student union. They offer free T-shirts and other gadgets to students willing to submit an application. The temptation is just too great for many poor college students. Then they get bogged down in credit card debt and must work to make the monthly payment. The increased time commitment interferes with their school work. One of our graduate students had borrowed so much money that she could not find a job upon graduation that would allow her to make her monthly debt payments and still have enough left over to live on. More and more of our students are finishing college with tremendous debt that compromises their life choices in many ways.

It may just be me, but I think that in these days of "easy money" via credit cards and loans, we need to re-evaluate our commitment to ourselves and our families. Is taking an expensive vacation worth the strain of paying for it after the fact? Is buying a new car worth five years of large car payments? In some ways, higher interest rates are a blessing since they at least cause us to reconsider taking out some loans.

The other downfall that many of us have regarding money is the opposite of racking up credit card debt. It is the idea of saving for a rainy day carried to an extreme. Some people are so tight with their money that they refuse to allow money to be a useful tool in their lives, thereby passing up opportunities to enrich themselves. I have one friend whose partner recently left her. She had lots of money (and when I say lots, I mean millions). However, one of the problem issues in the relationship was money. She became very angry when her partner, a master gardner, would go out and spend money on gardening supplies. The struggle over their finances became such a problem that it was ultimately one of the primary reasons for their split.

A balance or compromise approach with money is necessary in order for it to not be a constricting factor in our lives. My parents were of the Depression mentality. I thought they were a little too tight with their cash. My mother, to this day, refuses to carry any debt. She still "saves" for special occasions even though she has a rather large estate at this point in her life. What I like about my mother's approach to money is that it never became an either/and (fun OR money, fun AND debt). I can remember, when I was a child, her taking every extra dollar or two and putting them in a savings account which she used for special occasions. Once she had enough money in the account—about every six months or so—she would plan some fun event. She once took me to St. Louis for a Cardinals game and once to Kansas City to see the movie, *The Red Shoes*. The fact that she had to save for these trips became part of the fun. And at the end of the trips there were no credit card bills.

Jimmy

I knew Jimmy thirty years ago when he and my husband, Sam, were newly graduated from law school and in their first jobs working as attorneys for the federal government. Jimmy frequently confided to my husband that he wished he could take a little time out and be a beach bum. He just wanted to experience the joy and freedom of no responsibility for a brief period of time.

Jimmy's wife was the practical type and also somewhat traditional. (And, in actuality, Jimmy was too.) They bought furniture, eventually a house, she got pregnant, he went into private practice as an attorney, and his dream was never realized. But it was also never forgotten.

I lost touch with Jimmy and his wife after my husband and I moved and later divorced. However, just this year Sam told me that he had gotten a call from Jimmy, who was in town and wanted to meet Sam for a drink. Sam said Jimmy looks fine, maybe a little paunchier, that he has a very successful law practice, and that he and his wife have two grown daughters who are quite successful. Jimmy now is contemplating retirement. However, his wife wants him to keep working—he thinks she's worried that he'll be "underfoot" and in the way of her activities at home. At this point in his life, Jimmy could realize his dream of being that beach bum for six months, but somehow I doubt it. The joy has gone out of the fantasy. Maybe because he has that freedom now, or maybe because he waited too long. Sam recalled that Jimmy has an air of sadness in talking about his life. "Those times when we were younger were the best. Everything was possible then, except getting to be a beach bum," Jimmy said at one point. Had Jimmy and his wife been a little less focused on jobs, material possessions, and family when they were young, and had afforded themselves a brief indulgence by postponing the traditional lifestyle they had planned for themselves, Jimmy might have been a more fulfilled person when he met Sam for that drink. Or, maybe he would still be a beach bum.

All too often, we may sacrifice our dreams because we are either overly conservative (feel we need to save every dime) or underconservative (overspend every dime). If you can afford that beach bum fantasy, do it! If you can't, then here are some suggestions.

Financial counselors offer ideas that can be useful to all of us, whether we are close to bankruptcy, or just a little "overextended." I'm sure many of these tips sound familiar. But have you tried them? Doing so will allow you to more accurately assess your goals and plans without money problems being in the way.

• Don't charge anything that you cannot pay off within one month. You will feel at least psychologically that you can quit your job within thirty days.

• Build up your savings account. Have at least six months' worth of living expenses in the bank. If you quit your job, you have the assets necessary to survive for an extended period.

• Live below your income instead of above it. I know this means giving up all those things you like having: a new car, a new house, new furniture, etc. But the peace of mind that comes from knowing that your debt level is decreasing is ultimately much more satisfying to your mental state than amassing material goods. We are lured by advertising to believe that we have to have a certain standard of living and certain possessions in order to be happy. In fact, just the opposite is true. Having no debts is one of the best contributors toward happiness that I know.

• If you have to spend money, spend it on something that will provide a return, such as real estate. Boats, cars, and furniture depreciate in value.

Exercise

Financial Exam

Note: House mortgages are not considered in this exercise because they are essentially money-making versus money-spending loans. The value of your property is most likely increasing, making your home mortgage an investment.

1) How much money do you owe, apart from a house mortgage? Include car payments, credit cards, loans, etc. _____

2) What is your monthly net income?_____

3) What are your monthly living expenses?_____

   Do you allow for a little extra in your monthly living expenses (above) for unexpected expenses (car repair, house repairs, and medical bills)? Yes____ No____

   If not, refigure item 3, allowing for an additional 10 percent for emergencies, and enter the new figure there.

4) How much of the expenses in item 3 are going for the debt you listed in item 1?_____

5) At the rate you are paying those debts, how long will it take you to pay them in full, assuming you do not incur additional debt?_____

6) Are you willing to spend the amount of time it takes in item 5 to rid yourself of debt? (Don't forget, this probably means no new debt.)

Yes_____ No_____

If not, why? _____

9) How much money are you spending each month on interest (again, apart from a house mortgage)? _____ Just a reminder: this is your hard-earned money filling the pocket of creditors.

Take a look at your net income and determine how it is being spent on particular categories such as clothing, entertainment, luxury items, etc. You can determine your own categories, but try to make it not more than ten or so items and don't get too detailed. Include debts and interest:

Category	Amount

Exercise

Take Time to Reconsider

If you are experiencing financial difficulty, I'm willing to bet that your lifestyle image is as much determined by outside influences (advertising, parents, friends) as by your own wants, needs, and values. I'd like for you to take a moment to reconsider your lifestyle.

Think about what you value most in your life, tangibles as well as intangibles. Write down your top ten.

_____

_____

_____

_____

_____

_____

_____

_____

_____

_____

How many of the items in this last question match the items in number 9 above?_____

If more than 80 percent (eight) match, you are probably not experiencing serious money concerns that affect your work life. If you are at 50 percent (five), you may want to consider making some readjustments in how you spend your money in order to get it more in line with your values. If you are below 50 percent (four or fewer), you are probably experiencing significant incongruence in your external and internal values. This most likely is affecting your happiness both in your work and in your personal life. You may want to consider seeing a financial counselor or a personal counselor to discuss what you've learned from this exercise.

Chapter Seven Summary

On a scale of 1 to 5, with 1 representing "significant difficulty" and 5 representing "positive support," circle the number that best represents the influence of your finances on your career.

1	2	3	4	5
My finances contribute significantly to my career dissatisfaction.		My finances are a neutral influence on my career satisfaction.		My finances lend positive support to my career satisfaction.

"Perhaps now and then a castaway on a lonely desert island dreads the thought of being rescued."
—Sarah Orne Jewett

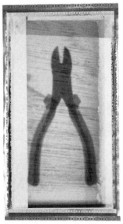

Chapter Eight

How's Life at Home?

"The family is the nucleus of civilization."
–Ariel and Will Durant

I supervise an excellent group of staff members in a university counseling center. They have been in their jobs for a number of years, are good at what they do, and are happy doing it. However, every so often one of them will seem to be having difficulty in his/her work. This dissatisfaction comes in a variety of forms: absent-mindedness, low motivation or lack of interest, conflict with another staff member, use of an unusually high number of sick days. Typically, I discuss my perception of the problem with my supervisor in an effort to determine what is going on. Is this staff member bored and in need of new challenges? Does he/she have the wrong responsibilities? Does he/she need some additional training? Is he/she competing with another staff member? While all of these things might be true and be sources of the problem, my boss always asks as his very first question: "Is this person having difficulty at home?" The first few times he did this, I tended to brush off his response and attributed the problems to the work setting. However, I started noticing that, in fact, the particular individual was having difficulty at home: a marital conflict, a financial problem, a recent death in the family. On most occasions, the "work problem" turned out to be a "home problem." This helped me to understand that sometimes there are outside causes for a drop in a person's performance level. By knowing that, I could support the employee instead of reprimanding him/her for his/her poor work performance. Certainly there are individuals with work problems which really are work problems. But often that is not the case.

Ben

Ben is an outstanding psychologist with twenty-five years of experience. He counsels college students, directs the clinical work of the staff, and trains doctoral interns who are preparing for careers in psychology. He is motivated in his work, reads the professional literature regularly, is highly productive, and gets along well with other staff. In short, he is an ideal employee.

Several years ago, although Ben was coming to work, it felt as though he were not there. He seemed remote and preoccupied. When I talked with him about his work, he seemed to have to bring it up to his consciousness. He forgot to follow through on responsibilities, he was unmotivated to start new projects, and he was a little grouchy with other staff. I interpreted this as boredom on his part. He had been in the profession for too long. Perhaps he was ready for a major career change. He had often talked about how he would like to be a farmer, and I assumed that he had finally given up on his current career and was either coasting to retirement or planning to leave soon.

Ten years later, Ben is still with the center, more vibrant and active than ever. He had been going through a long and painful divorce at the time, and his attention and energy were simply very tied up in an event involving children, the end of a long marriage, and complex financial arrangements. Once Ben was able to work through the divorce, he was back full steam. I'm glad that I didn't come down hard on him at the time. He needed the space and support to work things out in his personal life.

I don't know any working people whose job performance isn't affected by major problems at home. The trick is to recognize that the problem is a home problem, not a work problem. If you have been at your job for quite some time, are good at what you do, and suddenly find yourself having problems, be sure to take a look at home. You may be having difficulties there and are unaware of their effect on your work mood.

A colleague called me recently to say that she was looking for a new job. Could I help her with it? I asked if she was unhappy in her current job. She said that she actually liked her work, but that her boss had been being particularly hard on her lately; she did not want to endure his criticism any longer. I was perplexed since I knew that she was a valued employee by her boss. She had gone through a divorce a few years prior which had resulted in a very serious custody battle. In order to maintain full custody, she had felt it necessary to take off work early three days a week to be with her child after school. She had assumed that her boss would understand. She was both surprised and rather offended that he had difficulty with this arrangement. She felt he was being intolerant and unsupportive. Therefore, she decided to look for a new job.

In talking with my colleague, I pointed out that she is happy in her job, her boss does support her in many ways, and she may have difficulty getting off work three days early in any other job. She had been so absorbed in the issue of the custody battle and being "right" about it that she failed to see the effect it was having on her work place. I suggested a talk with her boss about a compromise before looking for a new job. She cooled down and did talk with him. I'm not sure of the actual arrangement, but I do know that she is still in that job.

If we are experiencing a crisis of some kind at home, of course it will affect our work. Unfortunately, in our culture we tend to divide work and home versus looking at the results of their interactions. I've sometimes found myself blaming my unhappiness on my work setting, only to realize a short time later that I was upset about events in my personal life. When I recognized the connection and focused on resolving the home problems, things improved at work. This method takes some patience for both you and your employer. But if you are a valued employee, most employers will provide you with the opportunity and support to figure out how to deal with personal matters. What does not help is to quit a job or make a major change in the work setting at the same time because then you lose the stability of the work setting and still have the personal concerns.

Exercise

Your Life Outside of Work

Take a look at your personal life.

1) Do you have close friends outside of work? Who are they?

_____

_____

_____

_____

_____

_____

2) Can you talk to them about anything that is bothering you?

Yes_____   No_____

3) Things that most bother you currently:

_____

_____

_____

_____

_____

4) Do you have a "significant other" who provides you with emotional support and to whom you also lend support?

Yes_____   No_____

5) Is this relationship going well?

Yes_____   No_____

6) Define what is going well or what is not going so well:

_____

_____

_____

_____

_____

7) Have you discussed the content of item 6 with this person recently?

Yes_____   No_____

If so, how did it go?

_____

_____

_____

_____

If not, why not?

_____

_____

_____

_____

8) Have you experienced a major loss of someone close to you recently (through death, relationship breakup, divorce, adult child leaving home)?

Yes_____   No_____

9) Who is this person? _____

10) If yes, have you had the opportunity to grieve this loss?

Yes_____   No_____

11) Have you lost a pet lately?

Yes_____   No_____

12) Are you in major conflict with anyone close to you?

Yes_____   No_____

13) If so, have you attempted to resolve it? If not, why not?

_____

_____

_____

_____

14) Are you in good physical health?

Yes_____   No_____

15) Have you had a check-up recently?

Yes_____   No_____

16) Are you worried about your physical health?

Yes_____   No_____

17) Are you experiencing serious financial difficulty?

Yes_____   No_____

18) If so, have you made an effort to find some solutions to these concerns?

Yes_____   No_____

19) Are you undergoing a significant change in your life in terms of your religious beliefs, concerns about aging, or philosophical meaning of life?

Yes_____   No_____

20) If so, have you sought help in looking at these concerns?

Yes_____   No_____

Note below any answers to the above questions that suggest an area that is causing you concern or difficulty. There are times when we assume that we can go on with business as usual even though we are undergoing a significant personal loss or problem. Allow yourself to spend some time simply identifying the concern(s) and focusing on how they are affecting your mental health:

_____

_____

_____

_____

_____

_____

_____

It is surprising how often we deal with concerns such as those above internally and on our own. We don't want to reveal our innermost worries and problems to others, and we think we can solve them by ourselves. But it is amazing how much it helps to talk about a deep inner worry with someone else, particularly someone we feel close to and who is supportive. Even seeking outside assistance from a financial counselor, doctor, psychologist, minister, rabbi, or priest can be extremely helpful. It is the "getting out" of the "inner worry" that helps. Try it. Keeping it inside only makes it worse and causes trouble, which you may not be aware of in all areas of your life.

Take a moment to write a plan for dealing with concerns that came to your attention in this chapter:

_____

_____

_____

_____

_____

_____

_____

_____

_____

_____

_____

_____

_____

_____

_____

_____

_____

_____

_____

Chapter Eight Summary

On a scale of 1 to 5, with 1 representing "significant difficulty" and 5 representing "positive support," circle the number that best represents the influence of your life outside of work on your career.

1	2	3	4	5
My personal life contributes significantly to my career dissatisfaction.		My personal life is a neutral influence on my career satisfaction.		My personal life lends positive support to my career satisfaction.

"Having a place to go—is a home.
Having someone to love—is a family.
Having both—is a blessing."
—Donna Hedges

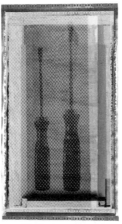

Chapter Nine

The Place of Volunteerism

"I don't know what your destiny will be, but one thing I do know: the only ones among you who will be really happy are those who have sought and found how to serve."
—Albert Schweitzer

Many of us make the mistake of looking at our careers as just what we do at the office—even if that office is in our home. When we look at our life in terms of segments (e.g., work from nine to five, dinner from six to seven, exercise from eight to nine, family time from nine to ten, etc.), we tend to miss the ways in which we can reconfigure some of our activities into very meaningful experiences. And by narrowing our perspectives in that linear way, we miss out on opportunities to enrich both our career and our personal lives.

In today's world of "busyness," one of the first things to go is a sense of service to others. We barely have time to take care of ourselves and our families, much less anyone else. We can't possibly imagine squeezing in yet one more thing to do or one more person with whom to share our energies. So, often we do not even consider volunteering as an option.

Why volunteer? In the past, certain volunteering experiences were cast into the areas of church work, pastimes for the wealthy, and activities for retired individuals. More recently, high schools and colleges have begun a new kind of volunteering called "service learning." Rather than look on volunteering as simply contributing one's time to assisting others in some way, students are encouraged to reflect on what they have learned as well. Students report a number of learning opportunities in volunteering, including understanding oneself and others better, building empathy skills, learning about diverse cultures, and improving communication skills. And nearly always, students report feeling better prepared to contribute to society as a result of the experience. This concept of volunteering emphasizes the benefits to both the giver and the receiver, thus getting away, to some extent, from the notion of paternalism often associated with volunteer activities.

Another advantage to service learning is that the volunteer activity is intricately tied to the rest of one's life rather than a separate entity. For a college student, service learning can be tied in with a particular class, a club or student organization membership, a career objective, or relationships with other students. By integrating volunteer activity into your life, you may be able to see the benefits increase significantly. No longer is donating time, skills, and energy something that you have to do "on the side."

If you are not involved in a volunteer activity, or if you are involved in a volunteer activity that does not enrich your career and your life, you might want to consider service learning. There are a number of ways to connect volunteer activities to your regular activities. Workplaces frequently provide opportunities to contribute to a charitable event. Certain organizations provide opportunities to volunteer in line with a set of professional ethics that reinforce positive character-building. Communities and religious institutions routinely offer opportunities for families to work on volunteer projects. Families or groups of friends can take up their own volunteer project as a way to spend time together enhancing their relationships while simultaneously providing service to others.

The point is that you can volunteer, even though you feel extremely busy. In fact, by volunteering you will probably find that you are happier. The trick is to know how to integrate service into the rest of your life in a meaningful way and to reflect on what you can learn from it. Volunteering has a subtle positive effect on our psyches. First, it takes our mind off ourselves. I've heard that one of the reasons why golf is so popular is that it is so mentally absorbing. It shifts our attention from our ruminations about our own problems to ruminating on that little white ball. In a way, volunteering does the same thing. It is a way of climbing out of your own self-absorption and taking a look at the larger world. In doing so, we often come to realize that there is real relief in not thinking about ourselves constantly.

Second, volunteer work provides opportunities for connecting with others. The common purpose of the work pulls people together, and since it is for a good cause, there is a sense of trust that comes with meeting people under these circumstances. Several faculty members and a group of our students once worked on a project where we cleaned up vacant lots and planted flowering trees. The grant that funded the project stated that we had to involve people in the neighborhood in completing our renovation. So, we invited the neighbors to join us in cleaning and planting. That day was truly special, not so much because of the trees (although they are still there), but because of college students working next to eighty-five-year-olds and five-year-olds to attain a common goal. Age, skin color, gender—none of that mattered. What mattered was getting those trees into the ground. And everyone contributed their time and their energy to work together!

A third benefit of volunteering is an opportunity to "give back" to your community. A while back, my mother received Meals on Wheels because she could no longer cook for herself, but wanted to remain in her own home. Daily, some kind person would come to her front door and deliver a hot meal. She enjoyed the person stopping by as much as the meal. I often felt a kind of wonder at the generosity of people who took care of my mother in this way. I couldn't have paid them enough—even if they had taken the money—to make up for the kindness of their acts. Just the other day I was reading an article about the Meals on Wheels Program in my own city. The article mentioned that the program was in debt and needing an "infusion" of cash. I happily made a financial contribution and plan to sign up for a driver's shift. This allows me the opportunity to perhaps provide for someone like my mother who could benefit as much as she did from that daily visit and hot meal.

Phyllis

Phyllis has a full-time job as a college counselor, is married, has one college-aged child, is active in her church, assists several elderly individuals who have difficulty taking care of themselves, and is president the local chapter of her African-American sorority. Needless to say, Phyllis is busy! However, she is rarely tired and just plain fun to be around. How does she do it? First of all, Phyllis and her husband assist the elderly individuals. This is something they have done together for many years. It has become a "ritual" within their marriage, and quite obviously their relationship benefits from the time they spend together helping others. Second, Phyllis' has a number of close friends who are in both her church and her sorority chapter. As a result, she and these friends cross paths often and are involved in several church and sorority projects simultaneously. This allows them to spend time together as friends and working together on mutual projects for the church and the community. In the process, they have fun together and support each other. Finally, Phyllis works with a number of inner city youth through her sorority chapter to encourage them to be successful in school and to provide them with self-esteem skills. She often "shepherds" a young inner-city youth through junior high and high school all the way to college. Since she is a college counselor, she knows what these girls need to do to prepare for college. Once they are in college, she can assist them with the adjustment and academic demands there. Phyllis has found a way to blend her family, friendships, church and community interests in ways that serve others, strengthen her relationships, and take advantage of her work skills. No wonder she is a happy individual!

Exercise

Volunteering/Service Learning

1) Do you currently volunteer?

Yes_____   No_____

If so, what are you doing?_____

2) Do you find this activity enjoyable?

Yes_____   No_____

3) Do you find that your life is significantly enhanced by this activity?

Yes_____   No_____

If so, how?_____

If not, how not?_____

4) If you would like to get involved in a volunteer activity,
   would you like to do this with:

_____friends

_____co-workers

_____family

_____church/synagogue

_____club or organization

5) What would you hope to accomplish by becoming involved in a volunteer activity, aside from the very important part of helping others?

_____

_____

_____

Here is a list of possible volunteer/service learning activities. Check those that appeal to you:

☐ Taking care of children

☐ Driving others to appointments/meetings

☐ Cooking for others

☐ Doing yard work or house repairs for others

☐ Building houses for others

☐ Providing flowers for those who are not well

☐ Picking up trash on roads

☐ Collecting clothes and furniture for those in need

☐ Assisting travelers at airports and train stations

☐ Visiting those who can't get out of their houses

☐ Reading to children

☐ Reading to adults

☐ Tutoring children

☐ Other_____

Take a look at the items that you checked. Then think about where you are currently in relation to volunteering and service learning. If you would like to develop this area of your life, write down a plan for doing so here.

_____

_____

_____

_____

_____

_____

_____

_____

_____

_____

_____

_____

_____

_____

_____

_____

_____

_____

Chapter Nine Summary

On a scale of 1 to 5, with 1 representing "significant difficulty" and 5 representing "positive support," circle the number that best represents the influence of volunteerism on your career satisfaction.

1	2	3	4	5
Lack of volunteerism contributes significantly to my career dissatisfaction.		Volunteerism is a neutral influence on my career satisfaction.		Volunteerism lends positive support to my career satisfaction.

Chapter Ten

"Be Prepared"

·"Do not call for black power or green power. Call for brain power."
–Barbara Jordan

The Boy Scouts were right. It pays to be prepared. In almost any endeavor, whether it is parenting, sports, or a performance, it is important to be current on the knowledge and skills associated with that area. For example, one of my favorite activities is biking. Within the past five years, a number of changes have occurred in both equipment and biking techniques that lend themselves to improved performance. Why would I care about this? By taking advantage of things such as lighter weight frames and new pedaling techniques, I can improve my performance and enjoy testing my skills. Plus, given my age of fifty-nine, the newer techniques help me to keep up with my younger biking colleagues!

In career preparation, there are always skills and abilities that can be used to help keep you current and marketable—and help to make work more fun. Just as in the sport of biking, having the most current knowledge and skills will improve your career performance and allow you to shift into new responsibilities or career changes if the opportunities present themselves. I recall being at a conference a few years ago and overhearing a conversation in an elevator between two colleagues of mine. One was saying to the other, "I can't wait to retire! I am tired of all the changes. I'll be rocking on my front porch by this time next year." The following year at the same conference I heard the news that that same director had passed away. Surprised, since he had seemed in good health, I inquired as to what happened to him. He did retire and then passed away quite unexpectedly a few months later. Who really knows what the cause of his death was, but I couldn't help but recall his elevator conversation. It was as if he had drawn a line about learning anything new. With that decision made, the only thing he had to look forward to was rocking on his porch. Not that there is anything wrong with porch rocking, but somewhere along the line he had lost his mental zest for learning—which may have affected his physical desire to continue living.

Being adaptable to new demands is helpful in our personal and professional lives. I was recently sitting in on job interviews of candidates for a position at our college. Two individuals were interviewed: one described herself as someone who takes orders very well and likes to be told what to do. The other one stated that she liked to be a "pathfinder" and look for the challenges and new opportunities in a job. Guess which one got the job? These days, the demands to learn in the workplace are tremendous. Two areas that seem to be the most demanding are technology and cultural diversity. Therefore, two particular areas of skills preparation lend themselves to improving one's general knowledge and performance in most career areas: computer skills and knowledge of different cultures. Expertise in these areas increases your chances of getting hired for a new job, getting promoted in a current job, and finding greater work enjoyment.

Computer Skills

This is the Information Age. Technology, especially via computers and the Internet, is causing vast changes in work and home life. Computers are being used in almost all manufacturing, fax machines and email have replaced "snail mail," and the Internet is the basis for access to an infinite amount of useful (and not so useful) information. Recently, I provided career counseling to an individual who is an assistant to a manager in a large manufacturing firm. She described how her boss had asked her to fax something for him. She did it, but she also let him know (very nicely) that most managers are capable of faxing their own information at this point. She could get away with this because she is right. The support staff (formally known as secretaries) in our office used to spend most of their time typing for the staff. Now, all of our staff do their own word processing on a computer, print out their own letters and envelopes, design their own programs, including PowerPoint presentations, and use email, voice mail, and Internet websites for most of their communications. The role of "secretary" has nearly disappeared. Support staff are now involved in more complex duties such as office flow and database management, budgeting and finance knowledge, and customer service. In order to be hired now as a psychologist or a support staff member in a counseling center, a person must have extensive computer skills.

Knowledge of Other Cultures

Partly as a result of advances in technology, the world is "shrinking." I'm reminded of this every time I fly. The number of individuals from foreign countries on any given flight increases each year. The first time I heard Japanese being spoken over the loud speaker in the Seattle airport I was surprised. This was probably ten years ago. Just recently, I noticed in the Denver airport that announcements are given in Spanish, Japanese, and English. We are all being exposed to people with very different cultural backgrounds from our own. If we don't know how to appreciate, respect, and converse with these individuals, we will not be successful, regardless of our chosen career.

A few months ago, I attended a workshop featuring as keynote speaker a man who was outstanding in his field—he had written one of the main books in his area, was quite well-known, and, following his early retirement, had become a consultant. Unfortunately, he had failed to keep current on cultural changes, particularly in the area of gender sensitivity. Although he thought he was being current and sensitive by remarking on the necessity of not becoming romantically involved with subordinates, those in the audience knew that this was "old news." His terminology, although perhaps appropriate seven years ago, was offensive to the majority of women in the audience. His expert knowledge was then questionable in light of his failure to keep current on a sensitive cultural issue.

It is possible to gain knowledge and information about different cultures and languages in a variety of ways. Traveling is one obvious means, if one likes to travel. However, the traveling needs to be interactive, preferably as a part of a study abroad program. Second, foreign films are now available at most video stores, and quality TV programming provides a picture of cultures in other countries and even differing cultures within our own. Language tapes are available for purchase or check out at local libraries, and community education offers classes in foreign languages. Fluency in another language is not necessary, though it can be tremendously beneficial to understanding a culture. By simply studying a language, one can become more knowledgeable about that culture.

Joe

As the Director of the Career Services Office, I regularly have luncheons with employers who are recruiting our students. On one of these occasions, I met with Joe, a recruiter from a large and well-known national accounting firm who was interviewing candidates for a highly competitive position. As usual, I asked the employer what qualities he looks for in a prospective employee. His answer surprised me. He said that in a recent search for a CPA position, he had narrowed the choice to two individuals. They were both very well qualified, but one clearly stood out. When I asked him why, he told me that this individual had studied abroad. I asked why having participated in a study abroad program would make someone more attractive for an accountant position. He said that this student's experience suggested that she was adventuresome, willing to take risks, and had exposure to a range of differing cultures. I could understand why an employer might prefer someone who had studied abroad for an international business marketing position, but I had not imagined that it would enhance an accounting major. However, it made the difference for this recruiter and the student he hired. And if it matters in accounting, it matters in most career fields. Employers appreciate that study/travel abroad makes people better employees and adds to the richness that employee brings to the work environment.

Exercise

Computer Languages

1) Have you used a computer with some degree of regularity during the last year?

Yes_____   No_____

If so, please check below to indicate for what purposes:

Computer Skill	Degree of Proficiency (Good, Average, Poor)	Level of Enjoyment in Using This Skill (Like, Neutral, Dislike)
Word processing		
Spread sheets		
Database management		
Email		
Internet		
Billing		
Graphic design		

2) Do you own a computer or have access to one through your employer?

Yes_____   No_____

3) Has it been purchased within the last three years?

   Yes_____   No_____

4) Does your work setting provide computer training?

   Yes_____   No_____

5) Does your local community provide classes in computer training?

   Yes_____   No_____

6) Have you considered taking a college level course in computer science?

   Yes_____   No_____

Exercise

Foreign Languages

1) Are you fluent in a foreign language?

   Yes_____   No_____

   If so, which language?_____

2) Have you ever studied a foreign language?

   Which language?_____

   Under what circumstances?_____

   Did you enjoy the experience? Yes_____   No_____

3) Do you travel?

   Yes_____   No_____

   If no, what prevents you?:

   ☐ Fear of the unknown?

   ☐ Lack of funding?

   ☐ Fear of flying?

   ☐ Other?_____

   _____

   _____

4) Have you ever traveled outside of the United States?

Yes_____   No_____

Where, when, and for what purpose?

How would you describe those experiences?

_____

_____

_____

_____

_____

_____

_____

_____

_____

_____

_____

_____

_____

_____

_____

_____

_____

_____

5) Have you ever lived in a location in the United States where the culture was very different from the one in which you grew up?

Yes_____   No_____

Where, when, and for what purpose? How would you define this experience?

_____

_____

_____

_____

_____

_____

_____

_____

_____

_____

_____

_____

_____

_____

_____

_____

_____

_____

_____

Go back and evaluate your skill level and your interest level in both the computer and foreign language/culture areas. If you feel both competent and interested in both areas, you are probably sufficiently skilled to have this area be of real benefit to your career. If you are not skilled, but have interest, I would encourage you to seek further training. If you are skilled but not interested, I would suggest that you look to other areas for career improvement, but keep in mind that these skills will serve you well. Therefore, you may want to at least keep them current.

Chapter Ten Summary

On a scale of 1 to 5, with 1 representing "significant difficulty" and 5 representing "positive support," circle the number that best represents the influence of up-to-date career skills on your career satisfaction.

1	2	3	4	5
Lack of up-to-date skills contributes significantly to my career dissatisfaction.		Up-to-date skills is a neutral influence on my career satisfaction.		Up-to-date skills lends positive support to my career satisfaction.

Chapter Eleven

Career Development: Issues of Age and Stage

"The greatest thing about growing older is that you don't lose all the other ages you've been."
—Madeleine L'Engle

Although we have not talked much thus far about the role of age in career satisfaction, certainly it can be a major factor. Actually, it is not age per se that is critical to career satisfaction since any of us can begin a new career at any time in our lives, health and other circumstances permitting. The issue of age is more an issue of career development. Although most of us enter our careers in our early twenties and "retire" in our sixties, some of us do begin new careers after retirement and end old careers having worked only a short period. Others of us may "step out" of a career to try something different for a while, have a family, or travel. Careers do develop, however, and if you are at the front end of your career, your perspective will be significantly different than if you are looking towards leaving. Knowing where you are in this process can help you to do those things that will make working more fun and rewarding. Let's take a look at a somewhat standard path for a career; of course it can vary according to the individual and the job.

Stage 1. Preparation

Preparing to enter a career typically consists of taking classes, earning degrees, doing apprenticeships, doing internships, and attending workshops.

Stage 2. Entrance

This stage consists of "getting your feet wet" in the career and proving yourself to others. It is typically characterized by tremendous learning, feelings of helplessness and inadequacy as well as mastering new tasks, and meeting others and making new friends.

Stage 3. Generativity

This stage consists of high productivity and can last anywhere from one to more than fifty years. In this stage, you feel competent and fully engaged in your career.

Stage 4. Reconsideration and Forks in the Road

This stage can occur at any point along the way and involves either leaving a career due to dissatisfaction, or making a change as a result of a new opportunity, promotion, or shift in responsibilities. Once you move to a new career or a new set of responsibilities, you return to Stages 1 and 2.

Stage 5. Master Level

This stage is characterized by high-level mastery of the career based on a wealth of experience and training. At this phase, you are often considered a senior, a mentor, a master, an elder, and are sought out for advice. There is considerable satisfaction in consulting work and in mentoring younger professionals. Actual production may not be as high as in the Generativity stage. The emphasis here is more on sharing knowledge.

Stage 6. Retirement from Formal Work

Some people never actually retire. They work until they are no longer able to, and they may be more than ninety years old. However, most individuals reach a point where they are officially no longer "working." At this stage in their lives they may shift their energies to a variety of activities. If they found working very satisfying, they may continue through consulting, becoming occupied in hobbies, volunteering, or engaging in other activities that provide learning and enjoyment. Some people may simply enjoy the rewards of a life of work well-done and slow down to "smell the roses."

It is important that you identify where you fit in these developmental stages. Each step has certain characteristics and carries with it certain responsibilities requiring varied levels of activity and commitment.

Sometimes, dissatisfaction in a career can have to do with a failure to recognize where you are in your career development. For example, Master Level individuals may still see themselves at the Generativity Level and not fully understand why people/colleagues are coming to them for advice and counsel. They may feel that they are not being productive enough, when, in fact, their productivity lies more in how they can teach others.

I was just recently asked to be on a panel of "senior counseling center directors." The purpose of the panel was for the "elders" to provide sage advice to the younger, less experienced directors. When asked to do this, I had that feeling of needing to look over my shoulder to see who the panel organizer was asking. It surely couldn't be me. First, I often feel as though I just entered this career yesterday and that I still have so much to learn. I continue to look for more of my "elders." And I wonder: is it possible that I have something to say of value to other directors? I feel competent in doing my job, but have I really matured to a point where I can teach other directors? Of course, my denial about age is an additional factor in all of this. Surely, there are many directors older than I am who could do a better job. But as I look around, I realize that I am one of the oldest directors. Oops! I guess I'm it.

The dichotomy between being seen as a master director and seeing myself in this role is a career development issue. My discomfort has to do with not accurately assessing my own development in my profession. As I become more comfortable with being in the role of a senior director, I can begin to actually enjoy the opportunity to be a mentor. I can comfortably move beyond the generativity phase of my career into a teaching/mentoring phase.

Entrance Level individuals who expect to know everything about a new job because they just completed an advanced degree in the area may get quite discouraged when they find they do not know everything, and thus they may feel inadequate. If they could understand that these feelings are normal during an early work experience, they might feel more comfortable in the job.

We have work-study students in our office, individuals who defray college tuition costs by holding jobs on campus. One young woman, who had been quite good as a student employee, was appointed to a "student manager" role. She trained her peers, set their schedules, and assigned their responsibilities. One of the other work-study students came in a few minutes late one day. The student manager (I think she had watched too many TV shows) fired the student on the spot for being late. It was clear to everyone except the student manager that she had overstepped her bounds of authority. She assumed that being a manager meant being able to fire people at her own discretion. Later, she had to apologize to the student and rehire her. It was a painful lesson for the manager. Had she considered her own newness and lack of experience in her position, she might have asked for direction before taking action. Our assumptions about our knowledge and authority when we enter a new job can be a cause of difficulty. It always is better to see ourselves as novices and ask questions frequently than to take actions on our own that later get us into trouble.

Knowing where you are in your development can help you in knowing what to expect and in finding increased satisfaction in your stage of work.

In order to assist you, here is a chart that describes the various stages and offers descriptions of their characteristics, challenges, benefits, and pitfalls of each. After locating your stage, become familiar with its various aspects.

Stage	Characteristics	Challenges	Benefits	Pitfalls
PREPARATION	Taking classes, earning degrees, doing apprenticeships.	Liking to learn, being open-minded, trying out new skills.	Having freedom and independence as a learner; exposure to interesting and challenging information.	Receiving little or no income. Disciplining oneself to complete studies and preparation.
ENTRANCE	Having many new tasks, being the newest employee, behaving professionally.	Getting used to the demands of a full-time job, feeling inadequate, seizing learning opportunities.	Receiving an income. Having opportunities to learn and try out this career. Getting to know new coworkers.	Feeling discouraged if job is too overwhelming. Job may not be a good fit.
GENERATIVITY	Engaging fully in a career with a high level of production.	Often requiring a significant time commitment and focus. Degree of production and accomplishment is important.	Receiving recognition for accomplishments and appreciation from employer and coworkers.	Experiencing burnout. Dealing with a difficult working environment. Balancing health, family, and work demands.
RECONSIDERATION	Leaving current career for a new career or change in responsibilities in current job.	Shifting back to Steps 1 and 2. Open to new learning and training with new responsibilities.	Getting into a career that is a better fit. New challenges in old career. Possible promotion and higher income.	Realizing that this new area may not work. Possible loss of income. Possible geographical move.
MASTERS LEVEL	Mastering the job at a high level. Looked to for training and mentoring.	Mastering tasks and responsibilities. A willingness to teach others and share knowledge.	Receiving recognition by others as a highly experienced professional. Opportunity to share knowledge with others.	Disliking being a "teacher." May have experienced burnout along the way and thus feel bitter about career.
RETIREMENT	Ending formal full-time employment.	Experiencing less structure, increasing opportunities for leisure activities and consulting.	Freedom that comes with less responsibility. New opportunities for learning and enjoyment. Time with friends and family.	Experiencing boredom. Lacking structure to create a sense of meaning. Receiving less income.

Exercise

Where Are You in Your Career?

Circle the step that best fits where you are currently in your career. Then re-read the Characteristics, Challenges, Benefits, and Pitfalls for that step and complete the following questions.

I see myself being in Stage _____ in my career development. I am _____comfortable_____not comfortable with the Characteristics, Benefits, Challenges, and Pitfalls of this stage. My discomfort has to do with the following (check any that apply):

_____thinking I am in a different stage than I actually am.

_____not liking the activities of the stage where I am.

_____experiencing serious Pitfalls at this stage.

_____finding the Challenges to be overwhelming.

_____not receiving sufficient Benefits.

Exercise

Plans for Satisfaction

Much of the difficulty in the Preparation, Entrance, and Reconsideration stages can be tolerated simply by realizing that the stage will not last forever. It typically is a means to an end. Much of the difficulty in the Generativity stage has to do with choice of a wrong career or a poor work setting. Difficulty in the Master stage can be dealt with through acknowledging your own expertise in the field and sharing it with others. Retirement dissatisfaction can often be dealt with by increasing your activities through a potentially new career area or pursuing hobbies and volunteer work.

My plan for increasing my satisfaction in my overall career development is:

_____

_____

_____

_____

_____

_____

_____

Chapter Eleven Summary

On a scale of 1 to 5, with 1 representing "significant difficulty" and 5 representing "positive support," circle the number that best represents the influence of the stage of your career on your career satisfaction.

1	2	3	4	5
The stage of my career contributes significantly to my career dissatisfaction.		The stage of my career is a neutral influence on my career satisfaction.		The stage of my career lends positive support to my career satisfaction.

"If you want a thing done well, get a couple of old broads to do it."
—Bette Davis

Chapter Twelve

It IS Just a Job

"To do good things in the world, first you must know who you are and what gives meaning in your life."
—Paula P. Brownlee

If you have tried to make your current job suitable to your needs and desires, yet you remain unhappy over a period of time, it is probably time to seek new employment. Because leaving an established career is very uprooting and time-consuming, I encourage you to try the least disruptive intervention first (making adjustments within your current setting) and the most disruptive intervention (changing job, career, location) last. However, if it comes to the big move, do it! Life is too short to be unhappy in your work. And after all, it is just a job, and you are not married to your work even though it may feel like it at times.

The next issue is: how to get out. Below, I've outlined some general steps to follow. Number of years worked, family commitments, education and training, and financial situation vary, so you may have to customize these suggestions. However, if you are contemplating changing careers, it will serve you well to learn about what is involved in making a good career decision.

We are all different, fortunately. We have different interests. We have different values. We have different aspirations. We have different physical constitutions. We come from different cultural and racial backgrounds. This is important to realize because it means that you need first to understand who you are before anything else. Fred Rogers of *Mr. Roger's Neighborhood* was right when he said each of us is unique. To base a career decision on other peoples' opinions of you, on what jobs are "hot," on what Uncle Harry did, on where you want to live, on what you wanted to be when you were sixteen could be a major mistake. Not that these things aren't important. But you must start with yourself.

If I were to point to the single biggest mistake people make in choosing a career, it is that they skip over this step and fail to take a careful look at themselves. In fact, it is this propensity to choose a career for all the wrong reasons that keeps those of us who are career counselors in the business. Probably about half of the college students who come in for career counseling in our center do so because they have chosen the wrong major. They may be sophomores, juniors, or even seniors, but they all show up with a very discouraged look on their faces saying that they just don't like "XYZ" as a major. It may be too boring, too difficult, too concrete, too abstract, but the underlying message is: "It is a wrong fit for me."

I place the blame for these confused individuals on our ambitious culture that rewards youth for early decisiveness. A high school student who says, "I'm going to be an engineer," is more highly admired by parents and teachers than one who says, "I don't know what I want to go into. I haven't made up my mind." Yet, we know that most sixteen- and seventeen-year-olds don't have the maturity or self-knowledge to make a permanent career choice. Hence, the number of students seeking assistance "down the road" after they have entered college and their choice of major has not panned out.

Significantly, at my center, we get not only college students coming in with concerns about career, we also get middle-aged adults, even a few "oldsters" who want assistance in finding the right choices and professional "fits." Although I wish they could have gotten on the right track earlier, I admire their willingness to come in for assistance. They recognize that career decision-making can be a complex process and that taking some time to think it through, even with a trained counselor, can provide very beneficial results. So, here is your chance to do just that. This is an abbreviated self-examination. I encourage you to see a career counselor and take a full battery of career assessments in order to get a more complete picture. Many colleges and universities offer this service for a reasonable fee, but this will help you to get started.

❦

Exercise

Interests, Values, Personality Traits, and Skills

Interests: List your ten favorite hobbies or activities and then check whether you have or would like to incorporate them in your job.

Hobbies/Activities	Available in my current job	Available in my ideal job

Personality traits:

Trait	Available in my current job	Available in my ideal job
I like working _____ with people in a team atmosphere, or _____ on my own.		
I like _____ being a leader, or _____ being a follower.		
I like_____ details, or _____ looking at the big picture.		
I like to learn _____ by doing, or _____ by reading about.		
I am a person who _____ uses logic in making decisions, or_____ uses feelings and personal values in making decisions.		
I like _____ structure and certainty, or _____ variety.		

Values. Rank the following from 1—10, 1 being most important.

Skills	Rank	Available in my current job	Available in my ideal job
Being recognized for what I do in my career by others is highly important to me.			
Being able to be challenged in my work is very important to me.			
Having a significant amount of job security is very important to me.			
Being able to work with people that I like and respect is very important to me.			
Having the opportunity to help others in my career is very important to me.			
Being able to learn new skills and information in my career is very important to me.			
Being able to be located where I want to be (geographically) is very important to me.			
My career is the most important part of my life.			
Having a significant amount of flexibility in my career is very important to me.			
Maintaining a high financial standard of living is very important to me.			

Skills: List both your natural talents (e.g., singing) and your learned skills (e.g., speaking a foreign language) here. Don't put down things that you don't like to do, even if you are good at them.

Skills	Useful in my current job	Useful in my ideal job

Once you have completed this exercise, go back over it and check those items that are feasible within your current job or, if you are just starting out, the job you are most likely to have. Then, think of your ideal job. (You may want to refer to the Future exercise in Chapter 2). Go over the above exercise and check those items that fit with your ideal career. Now, take a look at the list. How close are your present and your ideal careers? If they are close, you are probably in the right career area, possibly just not in the right setting. If they are very different, it's probably time to make a major change.

Exercise

Pinning Down Potential Careers

Go back again and take a look at the last exercise. It sometimes helps to do this with a friend or family member. Take a look at the whole list. Think of careers, including your ideal career, that mesh with your values, interests, personality traits, skills, and the future fantasy in Chapter 2. These may be careers that you have thought of already, or ones that may never have occurred to you before. (That is why it is helpful to have someone else, even a few others, do this part of the exercise with you.) Now, list those careers that best fit with your different qualities:

Potential careers:

_____

_____

_____

_____

_____

_____

_____

_____

Exercise

Time to Investigate

Now that you have some ideas about what might be the best fit for you, take a little time to research those careers. Here are some ways to gather information:

Go to your local library or bookstore and find books about specific careers.

Talk with anyone you know who is either in one of these careers or is close to someone who is in one.

Try an informational interview or a job shadowing experience. (Job shadowing involves spending an extended period of time, usually a half to a whole day, with a person at their job site, accompanying them through their routine job tasks. The intent is to gain on-site knowledge of the job.) Contact someone who is in the career of your interest and ask if you can either interview or job shadow him or her. If you just interview, this can be done on the phone or in person. Plan on about an hour. Job-shadowing is actually the best way to go because you have the opportunity to both interview the person and see the work setting.

Finally, the best way to find out about a potential career is to actually do a "trial run" through an internship. Many of the training programs at universities include internships in engineering, social work, teaching, and medicine, just to name a few. An internship allows you to "try on" the career, provides actual work experience, and tests job skills versus academic skills. More and more, people considering a career change try out part-time jobs or volunteer internships as a way to sample a career. Interning is time-consuming and not very profitable, but it does provide the very best test for measuring your match in a particular occupation.

As you are gathering information on careers of interest, keep track of what you have discovered on this chart. This will allow you to gather complete information and to make comparisons.

Career Research Chart: Note those careers that are of interest to you in the left column. Then indicate training required, annual average income, job market, duties and responsibilities, future prospects, flexibility, and learning opportunities in the additional columns.

	Career #1	Career #2	Career #3
Training required			
Annual average income			
Job market and availability			
Duties and responsibilities			
Learning opportunities			
Flexibility in schedule			
Future opportunities			
	Career #4	Career #5	Career #6
Training required			
Annual average income			
Job market and availability			
Duties and responsibilities			
Learning opportunities			
Flexibility in schedule			
Future opportunities			

Exercise

Obstacles: Now for the Realistic Part

We all have obstacles that make it difficult for us to follow a plan or prevent us from following it altogether. Stumbling blocks usually fall into the categories listed below. Rate yourself on each of them in order to determine how flexible you can be in pursuing a new career, especially since a change may require considerable investment of time and money.

1) My financial situation:

   Because of my current commitments, I have to make:

   ☐ more than I am making now.

   ☐ the same that I am making now.

   If it would be OK to make less, how much less? _____

2) My family commitments:

   Because of my current family commitments, I need to involve them in my career decisions:

   ☐ to a great degree.

   ☐ to an average degree.

   ☐ to a minimal degree.

3) Due to my future family commitments, I need to incorporate the following into my career decision making:

☐ children's expenses, including college.

☐ support of my partner/spouse.

☐ support of an elderly parent.

☐ allowance for sufficient savings in case I am incapacitated.

Learning/training: A new career or even a change within a career often involves new training or education. I have interviewed individuals who clearly do not want to receive any kind of additional training in order to make a career change. Then there are those who are wide open and are willing to take on several years of training in order to get into a career that suits them.

Where are you on the continuum?

No additional training |___| __|___|___|___| Several years of training

If you have significant others in your immediate life, how supportive are they of a career change for you? Since they are affected by any changes you make, their attitudes, support, and their own circumstances are very important to your decision. I interviewed a man recently who wanted to make a career change. He had talked it over very carefully with his wife and child. They decided that she would support the family for two years while he went to school. At that point, he would support the family so she could go to school. All three were willing to make the sacrifices necessary for them to live on one income for a few years.

Those closest to me:

☐ are very supportive of my need to get into a new career.

☐ somewhat supportive of my need to get into a new career.

☐ minimally supportive of my need to get into a new career.

Explain why for each item checked.

_____

_____

_____

_____

_____

_____

_____

_____

_____

_____

_____

_____

_____

_____

_____

_____

_____

_____

_____

_____

_____

Chapter Twelve Summary

On a scale of 1 to 5, with 1 representing "significant difficulty" and 5 representing "positive support," circle the number that best represents the influence of your knowledge of yourself on your career satisfaction.

1	2	3	4	5
Lack of knowledge of myself contributes significantly to my career dissatisfaction.		Lack of knowledge of myself is a neutral influence on my career satisfaction.		Knowledge of myself lends positive support to my career satisfaction.

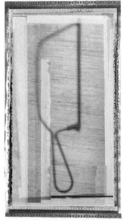

Chapter Thirteen

The Free Agent Concept

"Change is not made without inconvenience, even from worse to better."
—Robert Hege

Do you often find yourself angry with your employers because they are not giving you enough support? Do you think work would be better if only things were done "the good old way"? Your job dissatisfaction may be due to your lack of "free agency." Do you see yourself as an employee, or do you see yourself as your own boss regardless of whether you have an employer? Borrowing the concept of the "free agent" from baseball, Vonk and Hirsh in their chapter in *The Encyclopedia of Career Change and Work Issues* (1992), suggest that a "free agent" is someone who is in control of his/her career, skills, and contracts, and not beholden to a specific employer for success.

For many years, Americans have viewed themselves as being "taken care of" by their employers. If we simply do our job as we are told and do it well, our employer will make certain that we are paid and continue to be employed. This attitude toward work was most pervasive during the past fifty years. Employee loyalty was rewarded with company loyalty. Directions on how to work, what to do, and how to be successful came from above. More recently, the impact of technology, especially in the amount and availability of information, the downsizing of larger companies, the constant redefining of job responsibilities, and the diminishing importance of loyalty to employer/employee has caused a shift in what it takes to be successful in the work world. This is most obviously seen in the field of computer technology. Programmers change jobs and companies frequently, and they are constantly updating their skills either through their employer's training or through their own efforts. Their job responsibilities shift. Advances in technology make "the good old way" outmoded. Programmers and technicians are themselves valued primarily for the currency of their skills.

One result of these changes is increased responsibility placed on the individual worker. Rather than being able to rely on an employer for direction, training, and job security, individuals have to take on these responsibilities for themselves.

I have two dogs and a cat, and when I have to go out of town, I typically ask a college student to housesit. I have a couple of students that I use, but I always hope that Mary is available because she requires so much less instruction on my part. Here is Mary's style: I tell her that I will leave her a list of directions (that I have on my computer and that can be printed out each time I leave). The directions include such things as where the dog food is, when to feed the animals, the vet's name and phone number, and the name of a helpful neighbor in case of emergency. Mary says, "Fine." She may have a question or two—things that I probably forgot to tell her such as where I'll be leaving the key for her. I leave her a check on the dining room table, take off on my trip, and never worry for a minute about the house or the animals.

Sometimes Mary is busy, so I call Angela (a composite of all of the bad babysitters and housesitters I've ever had). She wants the job but sounds apprehensive. I remind her of the list of directions. She sounds even more apprehensive but insists that she would like the job. I ask if she has any questions, and she says, "No," but I get the feeling that is because she is unsure of what to ask. I leave the directions and a check for her on the dining room table, take off on my trip, and worry the whole time I'm gone.

When I return after Mary has been at the house, I walk in and can just tell that everything is fine. It is in the air, so to speak. Everything is in place. The animals look as if they didn't miss me for a minute. The sheets are washed and put back on the bed (not something I asked her to do, but greatly appreciated), all the dishes are clean, the mail is neatly stacked. There may be a couple of messages about repair people calling or friends who stopped by—all handled with a friendly confident style and appropriate information. One time, it was summer and it had been quite hot and dry. I failed to mention to Mary that the lawn needed watering, but of course, Mary took care of it.

With Angela, on the other hand, when I arrive home, I walk into the house and just know that things are not quite right. Angela appears with her continued apprehensive look and she tells me that she is sorry but she didn't know what to do when the washing machine broke (as she was doing her own laundry) and so there was some flooding in the basement. She also ran out of dog food, and didn't know what to do (I had forgotten to get a new bag before leaving. Of course, Mary would have just gone out to the store), so she fed the dogs table scraps, and they seem to be having digestive problems. The light bulb in the kitchen had burned out and was not replaced. The newspapers still sit in the front yard. Anyway, you get the idea.

The difference between Mary and Angela is that Mary sees herself as being in charge while Angela waits to be told what to do and only does what she is told to do. No creative problem-solving with her. She is guided by a narrow job description of specific duties. Which one would you hire? Which one do you think enjoys her job more? And this is not to say that Mary is smarter than Angela—they are both good students. The main difference is in the way in which they conceptualize their work and responsibilities. Being inflexible and too narrowly focused in a job these days can cause great difficulty, especially when we consider how rapidly worker responsibilities are changing.

Jeff

Jeff was the director of a community mental health clinic from approximately 1965 to 1990. The agency, funded by the county and state, provided psychotherapy to members of the community on a "pay what you can" basis.

Individual clients were seen for many counseling sessions. For the most part, there was no differentiation in amount of treatment based on diagnoses or degree of mental health disturbance. Individual therapists assessed how long their clients needed assistance.

Jeff was dedicated to his job and to his employer. He felt good about running an agency that provided help to the needy. He had a staff that was also dedicated to providing assistance to people who couldn't afford to pay very much (if anything) for counseling. Jeff was a nice guy, but maybe he was a little too comfortable in his role. His job responsibilities had not changed in twenty years. He could come to work, see the same staff members, greet the same receptionist, report to the same boss, and often even see the same clientele. In his mind, he was doing his job as he was supposed to.

Then along came managed health care and reform in the public mental health system. Almost overnight the entire system changed. Managed health care corporations limited the number of sessions that an individual could have and instituted rather strict reviews of counseling interventions and results. Public mental health funding shifted towards providing care for the chronically mentally ill versus for individuals who were experiencing a less devastating type of mental health issue. This occurred with very little warning and with very little instruction from those in management (i.e., the state and local governing bodies). Jeff was caught totally off guard. His old ways of doing his job were no longer effective. He found himself losing funding for the agency, battling with his employers, and fighting against "new-fangled" treatment regimens. He was so sure that the old way was right that he failed to take the necessary initiative to meet the new challenges. As a result, he found himself out of a job and feeling abandoned by his employer and the system.

What could have helped Jeff was a greater sense of needing to respond to a rapidly changing work world. Because he saw his employer as taking care of him and telling him what to do in order to be successful, he couldn't be a "free agent;" that is, he couldn't assess what he needed to do in order to survive the crisis.

Assuming you are not self-employed, the following exercise can help you determine if you are overly dependent for your career security on someone else.

Exercise

Who Do I Work for Anyway?

I expect the following from my employer. Check all that apply:

☐ To tell me when I need additional training for my job.

☐ To reward me for my loyalty to the company.

☐ To reward me for my longevity with the company.

☐ To provide me with clear direction as to what is involved in my job and how to do my job.

☐ To advise me on how to be promoted.

☐ To advise me on how to be successful at what I do.

☐ To provide me with job security.

☐ To provide me with an adequate income.

☐ To tell me where my future lies with the company.

☐ To provide me with adequate benefits (i.e., health care, vacation time, and pension).

_____TOTAL

If you have checked more than five of the above, you might want to consider that at least some of your work unhappiness is due to expecting your boss to be your boss—telling you what your job is, making sure you are doing your job, and preparing you for what is to come in your job future.

Exercise

Be a Free Agent

The following actions can help you to be in charge of your work life. In becoming a "free agent," you will feel a greater sense of control over your future and gain a greater sense of security.

1) We have already talked about this, but it cannot be emphasized too much: train, train, train. Don't wait for your employer to tell you to polish or learn a particular skill. You need to figure out what you need to do to remain competitive.

2) Don't "rest on your laurels." In business, memory is very short. The person who can do the job gets the job.

3) Don't assume that because you are working hard, you will be rewarded. It is what you do, not how hard you work, that counts.

4) Be flexible in the way you look at your job. Don't assume that because you did such and such last year you will be doing the same next year. Be open to change.

5) Take initiative. Often, things are changing so fast, the work appears before the job is created. If you see that something needs to be done, do it. Be willing to work outside of your job description and pick up the slack where you see it.

6) Keep current on job trends in your field. Again, things are changing fast, and for all you know, your job may even be eliminated. There are a significant number of careers such as typist and phone operator that have almost vanished in the past few years. Make sure that you are in an area that is not about to become extinct.

7) Don't rely on your employer for your future security. This goes for vacation, retirement, health benefits, and all of those other perks that we assume will go along with our jobs. Figure out a way to save for yourself: become your own benefits manager.

8) Don't rely on having your current job in the future. Again, in today's world, people are changing careers frequently. Have a back-up plan. Consider the following question: If I lose my job in six months, I will:_____

_____

9) See this new way of looking at employment as a free agent as being positive because it is. Free agency will provide you with much greater job satisfaction and a sense of fun and excitement over future possibilities.

10) Avoid being a "Jeff" by fighting for the old ways of doing things. They are long gone.

Chapter Thirteen Summary

On a scale of 1 to 5, with 1 representing "significant difficulty" and 5 "positive support," circle the number that best represents the influence of the concept of "free agent" on your career satisfaction.

1	2	3	4	5
Not using the free agent concept contributes significantly to my career dissatisfaction.		The free agent concept is a neutral influence on my career satisfaction.		The free agent concept lends positive support to my career satisfaction.

"I don't know anything about luck. I've never banked on it, and I'm afraid of people who do. Luck to me is something else: hard work and realizing what is opportunity and what isn't."
—Lucille Ball

Chapter Fourteen

Putting It All Together

"The future belongs to those who believe in the beauty of their dreams."
–Eleanor Roosevelt

Here is your chance to put your "big picture" together. Remember, there are no rights or wrongs. Instead, think of this chapter as providing an opportunity for you to get some information and direction on how to fix your career. You will most likely see some highs and some lows. That is typical. You may have only one or two highs and a bunch of lows. Or the reverse may be true. You may find that you have your career concerns more together than you had thought. On the other hand, you may have discovered that there are a number of areas where you need to take action. Regardless, you should feel much better about how to achieve a more satisfying career.

The good news is that you now have a better understanding of yourself in relationship to your work. Finding the problem is half the problem and half the solution. I have a friend who says that when she has car problems, she just assumes that she will have to take her car in at least three times before it gets fixed. That way, if it only takes one time or two times, she's happy. Getting the right diagnosis of what is wrong with your car or your career is critical to getting it fixed. Once you have the diagnosis from the exercise below, fix the problem. It probably won't be as difficult as you might have imagined. The following assessment will help you to determine your degree of career satisfaction and identify areas that detract from it. Filling in your scores will give you an opportunity to focus on those areas that need some attention and also to continue in those areas that are most supportive of your happiness.

From your summaries at the end of each of the chapters, take your ratings and place them on the assessment chart below.

Career Satisfaction Assessment

Clear Out the Cobwebs (Chapter 1)   Score_____

Choose a Career As You Would a Lover (Chapter 2)   Score_____

Stuck Doesn't Have to be All Bad (Chapter 3)   Score_____

And You Thought It Was about the Job Itself (Chapter 4)   Score_____

If You're Not Having Fun, Lower Your Standards (Chapter 5)   Score_____

Moving—It's More Than Renting a U-Haul (Chapter 6)   Score_____

Save for a Sunny Day (Chapter 7)   Score_____

How's Life at Home? (Chapter 8)   Score_____

The Place of Volunteerism (Chapter 9)   Score_____

"Be Prepared" (Chapter 10)   Score_____

Career Development: Issues of Age and Stage (Chapter 11)   Score_____

It IS Just a Job (Chapter 12)   Score_____

The Free Agent Concept (Chapter 13)   Score_____

Total Score_____

Total Scores

- Scores over 50 suggest a strong degree of career satisfaction.
- Scores between 35 and 50 suggest moderate satisfaction but a need to look at specific areas that might need improvement.
- Scores between 25 and 35 suggest that there are critical problem areas needing immediate attention.
- Scores below 20 suggest strong dissatisfaction in your career—but you probably already know that!
- Use the assessment to focus in on those areas that need improvement. In this way, you can "fix" the areas that are causing you the greatest career dissatisfaction and leave the others alone.

New Horizons

Many times we know we are unhappy about something in our lives, but we can't pinpoint exactly what it is. We either avoid taking a look at what is wrong or we identify the wrong thing. Part of the intent of this little book is to assist you in defining for yourself what "works" and what doesn't in your career life. By taking a closer look at the specific areas addressed in this book, you have been able to get a handle on those things that are either bothering you or are being positive supports for you. I strongly encourage you to take this information as a "beginning." Do something with what you have learned. Try out some new activities in those areas where you are least happy. A friend of mine has a private social work practice (when she isn't raising horses). When I asked what "theoretical approach" she uses with clients who are unhappy in their lives, her response was straightforward and clear: "I just tell them to do something different."

"If one advances confidently in the direction of their dreams, and endeavors to lead a life which they have imagined, they will meet with a success unexpected in common hours."
—Henry David Thoreau

Good luck to you in your life endeavors!

About the Author

Diana Pace is a licensed psychologist, Director of the Career Planning and Counseling Center at Grand Valley State University (Allendale, Mich.) and an adjunct faculty member at GVSU. She earned a B.A. in history from Duke University, and an M.A. in counseling and a Ph.D. in counseling psychology from the University of North Dakota.